# The Dukkawa of
# Northwest Nigeria

A Dukku man of some standing.

African Series Volume 5

# THE DUKKAWA

## OF

# NORTHWEST NIGERIA

by

## CESLAUS PRAZAN

EDITED WITH ADDITIONAL NOTES BY
D.J.M. MUFFET, O.B.E.

Line Drawings by
Mary Smith

## Duquesne University Press

PITTSBURGH
Distributed by Humanities Press, Atlantic Highlands

Library of Congress Cataloging in Publication Data

Prazan, Ceslaus, 1936-
    The Dukkawa of northwest Nigeria.

    (Duquesne studies: African series; v. 5)
    Includes bibliographical references and index.
    1. Dukkawa (African people) I. Title. II. Series.
DT515.42.P7      309.1'669'5      77-365
ISBN 0-391-00655-X

*First Edition*

For

**Louis and Lillian Prazan**

# ACKNOWLEDGEMENTS

My grateful thanks are due especially to Rev. Peter Martin Otillio, O.P. We have worked together for eight years among the people of the Dukku tribe and the information contained herein is as much his as it is mine.

Also to Valerie Worsley, B.B. Waddy, Georges Festinger, Stephen Kajang and all the others too numerous to mention who have helped me in any way, as well as to Amanda Muffett, who typed the final draft.

A special word of thanks to David Muffett for his editorial forward and notes.

Ceslaus Prazan, O.P.

# CONTENTS

# ILLUSTRATIONS

# EDITORIAL
# FOREWORD

This is not a *scientific* book. Some people might even claim that it is not a *scholarly* book, though I personally would disagree fundamentally with them on that score. But what no-one can possibly deny is that this book is a humanistic book, which deals with the values, aspirations, endeavours, and day to day frustrations of the people with whom it is concerned with sympathy and understanding and with dignity and humility. It is this last attribute, in particular, which makes the book, for me at any rate, an exceptional work and a valuable one.

It is probably true that we of the western world in this last quarter of the twentieth century know less and understand less about the working of a tribal society (or even of an extended family) than mankind has at any time before in history. Because of the pressures of our modern society, because of the fragmentation and dispersion which so often results from enhanced job mobility, because of "the generation gap", of "adolescent alienation", or even, so some would say, because of the malignant influence of the T.V. set, "Family" as the word is currently understood, bears but little resemblance (in general terms) to its meaning of a mere fifty years ago, and practically none at all to what it meant in 1776.

If this is the case with "Family", however, how much more so is it the case with "Tribe". Western Man's understanding of the concepts and values which pertain to that word and to its associated cluster in the language has been so debased as positively to have been perverted.

Nor is ignorance the only factor that has contributed to this lamentable situation; prejudice also has played its part as well. Thus, because of the basic ignorance of the subject from which xvi The Dukkawa of Northwest Nigeria

many otherwise competent and even prestigious commentators have suffered on the one hand, and because of the insatiable urge of the news media to create a sort of shorthand of code words to encompass concepts which otherwise are considered to be too sensitive to be dealt with openly on the other, the word "tribe" and its adjective "tribal" have recently assumed all the connotations of dirty words (indeed, almost of obscenities), and the concept of the tribe as a social institution has been similarly demeaned. But no word has been more uniformly prostituted than has "tribalism".[1]

In terms of its currency in the language, it is a relatively recent acquisition, and in its original meaning it is almost impossible for any exception to be taken to it. Nowadays, however, it is made the subject of the same unthinking blanket of opprobrium which is uniformly applied to many other of the "isms" which are so commonly bandied about.

That all this should have occurred at a time when and in a society in which "ethnic" and "ethnicity" have been elevated to an almost spiritual exhaltation is not really the more remarkable. It is merely a clear manifestation of the prejudicial element previously referred to and of that peculiar double standard which for centuries has bedevilled western culture — the very fact, indeed, which gave rise to the need for the newsmedia code words in the first place.

Thus, according to these standards, "Ethnic", "Ethnicity" and "Ethnological" are "good" or "laudable" or "understandable", whilst "Tribe", "Tribal" and "Tribalism" are "wicked" or "savage" or "native" (itself a much abused term). What is never openly acknowledged, of course, is that the word "Ethnic" and its derivatives are *only* ever used in connection with Western Civilization (so called) and even then usually only for the purpose of indicating differences among *whites*, whilst "Tribe" and "Tribalism"

---

[1] According to the O.E.D., the word first gained currency c. 1886, being used in that year in the *Edinburgh Review*. It is defined as "The condition of existing as a separate tribe or tribes, tribal system, organisation or relations". Thus the word is much less ancient than *tribe* itself (1250), and is also considerably younger than *liberalism* (1819), *radicalism* (1820), *socialism* (1832), *conservatism* (1835), *communism* (1843), and *nationalism* (1844). *Racialism* is dated as 1907 (the word *racism* or *racist* does not occur at all) and first appeared in the *Daily Chronicle* of that year. It is defined as "Tendency to racial feeling; Antagonism between different races of men". It is this connotation which has been ascribed by the ignorant to *tribalism*. (Ed.)

are only applied to non-Western (and therefore "backward", "un-civilized", or "underdeveloped") situations.

The fact that these two word systems mean exactly the same thing is conveniently overlooked, even though the fact, also, that there is only one word in the language for "the study of tribal or racial difference", and that that word is "Ethnology", so signally emphasises the truth of the matter.

Sooner or later, the propensity for so called experts to pervert the language will have to be called to a halt. Such practices are, of course, inherently evil, as George Orwell pointed out. That Western man has so carelessly indulged in them is a condemnation not so much of his intellectual inadequacy in dealing with the frustrations and insecurities of the societies he has created, as it is of the paucity of the *value system* which underlies those same societies, as well as of the utter incapacity which most academicians have so patently displayed for incorporating *value* as an element in their analyses of political or social reality.

Well does the writer recall the insistence on "value-free judgement" which was so typical of formal American scholarship when first he came in contact with it. That this was nothing more than a protective reflex left over from the days of Senator Joe McCarthy (or, indeed, that it still had "standby capability" as a "cop-out" in the face of renewed activity of that nature) was never admitted for a moment. Nor has the fact that such intellectual schizophrenia has led directly to Watergate and to the plethora of Corporate, Executive and Political corruption with which that whole episode has become indelibly identified received its due recognition either. Nor, simply because so many African politicians and academicians have joined in the general condemnation of tribal values, is the situation made any different: Such thoughtless subscription to self-denigration does them little credit.

Now, however, Ceslaus Prazan has written a book dealing with a tribal people which brings out *their* value systems, *their* ethos, *their* sense of intrinsic human worth, in a manner which is truly remarkable. Much of what the author writes ought to make the proponents of many Western values (at least, of those which have so exclusively an acquisitive intent) pause in their progress, consider a moment, and perhaps even hang their heads in shame.

That this book was written by a missionary (and a dedicated and committed one at that) may therefore appear at first sight to be quite extra-ordinary. Heretofore, indeed, no class of persons has been more active an agent in the Western acculturation process than that of Missionary Societies and Orders.

But such a judgment, in the context of the Order to which the author belongs, would be completely facile. No-one who has stood, as the writer has stood, in the simple but incredibly beautiful mission church in Malumfashi and wondered almost in awe at the genius that dictated that the tabernacle in which the consecrated communion breads are kept should be a simple everyday *rumbu* (cornbin), thus truly conjoining necessity with symbolic propriety, or that the altar rails should be made up of the ubiquitous household pestle and mortar, can fail to have had brought home to him most vividly that he was witnessing a new beginning and that here at last might be a vehicle for the propagation of the Christian Faith which would seek identification with and not superiority over, the cultures with which it came in contact. The contrast between that Chapel in Malumfashi and the "corrugated Gothic" or "concrete Perpendicular" of earlier days is not casual. It is fundamental, and it represents a change in attitude that many who have known Africa well have insisted would have to come, and the final advent of which they can only welcome, whilst fervently hoping for its rapid extension into many of the realms of contemporary scholarship, the arrogance of which is often monumental.

Perhaps this change in attitude is best summed up in a remark which the present Bishop of Sokoto, The Most Reverend J. Michael Dempsey, O. P., made to the writer just before his appointment to that high office in 1967. "We need" he said, "to begin a dialogue with all the people with whom we work, whether they be Moslems or Animists, and we should try to build on what we find there without destroying what they have. God's grace is working in them, and whatever is good in their traditions and values should merit our respect. For generations they have endured and have much of excellence in their beliefs and customs."[2]

It is clearly in the spirit of this same ideal that the author has approached his own work, and the result is illuminating.

In terms of the general history of African Mission Societies, the involvement of the Dominican Order in Northern Nigeria is a recent one, and it was not until 1951 that Father Thaddeus Lawton

---

[2] The Bishop expressed similar sentiments at his consecration. See *Dominician Life;* Vol. 11, No. 3, Autumn, 1967. (Ed.)

undertook a fact-finding visit and, in company with Fr. Watson SMA (Societé des Missions Africaines), whose Society had done initial missionary work there, visited Sokoto, in which Province the Dukkawa reside. The upshot was that in January of 1952, the Prefecture of Sokoto and Katsina was formally established, and in 1954, Monsignor Lawton became the first Prefect Apostolic. He was consecrated the first Bishop of Sokoto on 15 August, 1964.

The first known Catholic (and indeed Christian) contact with what is now the diocese, however, began in 1688, when the Belgian Franciscan Brother Pieter Fardé managed to engineer his release from captivity in Agades, and journeyed southwards, leaving behind him two hundred baptised slaves (including almost certainly the first Hausa Christians) in the care of two newly arrived Priests who had also been enslaved.

Brother Pieter did no more, apparently, than pass through the then autonomous (or at least semi-autonomous) Hausa Kingdoms of Gobir, Katsina, Zaria and Zamfara on his way to the great political and commercial center of Kano. At this time, Kano was ruled by the thirty-sixth King of the dynasty, Dadi son of Bawa (1670–1703). Early in his reign, the Jukun had actually breached Kano's walls and entered the City, only being ejected after a hard fight.

In 1710, two other Franciscan Priests, Fr Carlo and Fr Severino de Delisia journeyed from Tripoli to Bornu and then on to Katsina. They were seeking the Kingdom of the Kororofa (the Jukun), whose ruler was reputed to be a practising Christian.[3] Both of them died in Katsina in August, 1711. In this expedition, no doubt, there was more than a trace of the urge to seek out the by now legendary and mythical Prester John. No other priest seems to have come into the diocese until 1921, when Father Carminatti, SMA. rode his bicycle the 250 miles from Zaria to Sokoto. It is, however, from the appointment of Monsignor Lawton as Prefect that the Dominicans' apostolate took on a life of its own. In 1958, the Order extended its activities to Yelwa, the headquarters of the Emirate of Yauri, one of the ancient Hausa Kingdoms numbered not among the founding *Hausa Bakwai*[4] but

---

[3] For details of this expedition see R. Gray: "Christian Traces and a Franciscan Mission in the Central Sudan 1700–1711," *J.A.H.* Vol. VIII, No. 3, 1967, pp.383–393. At the time Kano was loosely under the overlordship of Bornu. *(Ed.)"*

[4] The original "Seven Hausa" were Daura, Katsina, Gobir, Biram, Kano, Zegzeg (Zaria) and Rano. The *Banza Bakwai* are Zamfara, Nupe, Kebbi, Gwari, Yauri, Yoruba and Kororofa. At least, that is what the Hausa themselves say! (Ed.)

among the *Bunza Bakwai* — the Associated Seven — which together with them formed the original components of the Hausa
language/culture, and it was here that Father Prazan began his
work with the Dukkawa.

Father Prazan's acquaintance with the Dukkawa began just
about ten years after my own first encounter with them, which
had occurred in the summer of 1947, when, as a newly joined
Cadet in the Colonial Administrative Service, I was posted to
Yelwa to supervise the annual cattle count on the Yauri/Kontagora
border. This is, *par excellence,* Dukku country, with the nomad
Fulani, the *Bororoji,* merely super-imposed on it by virtue of their
temporary occupation of their *mashekarai.*[5] Be it admitted that I
fell unashamedly in love with both!

It was always said in the Service that one's first appointment
remained *the* great experience of one's life, and this was certainly
true of myself and Yauri. From that most magnificent of mentors,
the Emir Abdullahi, whose son now rules, I learnt more about
Africa in a week than I would otherwise have done in a year. His
gracious, wise, yet always strictly pragmatic approach was positively inspirational, and he remained my firm friend for life, one
whom I never ceased to consult at every opportunity. He it was
who drove me in his own car to the nearest doctor when I was
stricken with infective hepatitis when down beyond the Molendo
River, over eighty miles away and had to ride alone for three days
to get back to the nearest outpost of "civilization". I arrived at the
Yelwa Headquarters of the Sudan United Mission[6] about noon
one Sunday, filthy, unkempt and utterly exhausted, convinced
that I was going to die, for I believed I had contracted Blackwater
Fever. This was a disease of dreaded memory, from which no-one
ever recovered save by a  miracle. It is a measure both of my then
youth and of my ignorance that I should have made this diagnosis,
for "blackwater" was (though not so recognised at the time that it
was wreaking its principal havoc) nothing more than acute quinine
poisoning, and since I had never taken quinine in my life, the syn-
thetics being that much more effective, as well as being, in this respect harmless, it was quite impossible that I could have developed
it.

---

[5] Wet-season grazing grounds. (Ed.)

[6] There to be taken in by that most practical of Christians Mrs. Edma Brubacher,
a Canadian from Kitchener, Ontario, who nursed me and cossetted me until transport
could be organized, for the roads then were awful. (Ed.)

The major symptoms of hepatitis, are, however, much the same, and I can plead this in extenuation, but anyway, to be convinced that one is about to die alone and under those circumstances is a gruesome and terrifying experience in itself, and friendship offered on such occasions is doubly to be treasured. In those days too, hepatitis was simply "just jaundice", and by the time I got to Sokoto, I was regarded as cured, with only ten days sick-leave allowed to convalesce in Jos, so I was soon back in Yauri. But whether it was the Government Resthouse (with the Emir's own refrigerator carried up there and installed before one's arrival by his personal instructions) or a Dukku *tunga* near Bakin Turu or Giro, the same warmth of affection and hospitality was always present in Yauri, even among the *Bororoji* whose main ambition in life was to hide the number of their cattle in order to avoid paying tax on them!

Thus it is that to be asked to assist in the production of Father Prazan's text is not only a pleasure in itself; it also constitutes a measure of debt-repayment on my part, repayment for sharing lives and for common experiences which the Dukkawa shared with me and which I shall never forget.

One serious problem which did arise in the preparation of the final text concerned the method by which the Dukkawa should be described. *Dukkawa* is really a Hausa word meaning "the people of Dukku", and it is plural.[7] The true name of the tribe, therefore is Dukku, and the singular noun, the Hausa idiom still being employed, would be *BaDukku* meaning "a man (or woman) of the Dukku tribe". Repeatedly to write of "the people of the Dukku tribe" or of "a woman of the Dukku tribe" would be both awkward and prolix. Advantage was therefore taken of the Hause collective *Dukkawa* and this has been used throughout wherever a sense of "the people of the Dukku tribe" is intended.

At the same time, since the word is already plural, its further pluralization as in *"Dukkawas"* would be quite improper. Where such a sense is desired to be conveyed, the appropriate phraseology is "Dukku men" or "Dukku women". As has been pointed out

---

[7] The suffix *awa* in Hausa (sing. the prefix *Ba*) is used to denote "a man of the ...." in the singular, and "people of" in the plural. Thus *BaYarabe, Yarabawa,* or, *BaNinge, Ningawa* etc. Sometimes the arrangement is slightly irregular, as in the case of the Hausa themselves *(BaHaushe, Hausawa)* and sometimes the singular form varies according to sex, e. g. *BaFillace,* a Fula man, *BaFillata,* a Fula woman, the plural for both sexes being *Fillani.* (Ed.)

above, however, there is also a singular personification available from Hausa, and on occasions, both for variety and for clarity the word *BaDukku* will also be found to appear in the text.

Another complication regarding the Hausa language is implicit throughout. It is one, moreover, which the author has added to rather than relieved. He has, however at least gone partway to recognising it.

Hausa, he acknowledges, is the *lingua franca* which supervenes over much of the north of Nigeria, including the area inhabited by the Dukkawa. But he, regrettably, has given no indication of the extent to which it has permeated Dukku culture and "invaded" the Dukku language in the form of loan-words.[8] This is a serious defect, especially when it is remembered that every single word but *gormo* which Father Prazan uses to describe Dukku practices is standard Hausa. It must be remembered, of course, that he would be using Hausa and not *Dukkanci* as his vehicle of communication, but it would have been valuable to have arrived at some opinion as to the capacity of the Dukku language itself to withstand assault from the dominant social, cultural and economic influence which is undoubtedly Hausa.

Since the Hausa terminology *is* so widely employed by the author, however, it is as well to clarify somewhat the rules which must govern its usage. This is especially the case concerning plurals. Hausa commonly has two distinct plurals, the "plural of scarcity" and the "plural of abundance". In many cases, the plural of scarcity employs the singular form, without any variation. Thus, the word *Biki* (feast, festival, ceremony, gathering or party) can denote one single event or a collection of them. Thus, it is proper to write about *a Funeral Biki* in connection with a single event (e. g. "A man attending a Funeral *Biki* will usually go. . . .etc".) and of "Funeral *Biki*" in a collective sense (e. g. "Funeral *Biki*" play a large part in. . . .etc."). If this simple rule is borne in mind, no especial difficulty is likely to be encountered. What can never properly be used, however, is a phrase such as "Funeral *Bikis*", or some similar bastardization of the two languages.

---

[8] From personal experience, I know this to be considerable, and this view is confirmed by studies undertaken of neighbouring groups such as the Gungawa, also of Yauri Emirate. See Salamone F. A. "From Gungawa to Hausa or 'I'd Rather Switch than Fight'" — An Example of Ethnic Identity Change," presented to the 16th Annual Meeting of the African Studies Association at Syracuse, 1973. *(Ed.)*

Practically nothing has been written about the Dukkawa.[9] Early in the formative years of Nigeria there were a few notes made. To these Father Prazan sometimes refers, not always in terms of approbation. One or two references can be found in modern ethnographies, but they are rather scrappy and do not contribute much. Father Prazan's book therefore is the first attempt at a study in depth.

Throughout the book, my own part as Editor has been limited to some minor textual corrections and to the contribution of what I hope are helpful footnotes. In order to distinguish what I have written from Father Prazan's own, I have added to mine the code (Ed.), and for their inaccuracies, if any, I most humbly apologise.

But for Father Prazan, who was once a student of mine and to whom I taught the rudiments of the Hausa language and (I hope) imbued with some of my own enthusiasm for Yauri, no apology is needed, or ought, indeed, be contemplated. No doubt much has been omitted, and a great deal more needs to be amplified. Nothing, I am certain, of what is reported here, is inaccurate or has been tampered with. It comes to us, like Cromwell's nose, "warts and all". But like Cromwell's nose too, that is part of its beauty!

D. J. M. M.
Institute of African Affairs,
Duquesne University,
Pittsburgh, Pennsylvania.
January, 1976.

---

[9] Meek makes practically no reference to the Dukkawa. Apart from those authorities mentioned in the text, the only other available data is contained in Salamone F. "Structural Factors in Dukawa Conversion"; *Practical Anthropology,* 19 (1972): pp. 219–225, and, if I remember aright, in the now completely unobtainable *Provincial Gazeteer of Sokoto Province,* by P. G. Harris. The same author's "Notes on Yauri (Sokoto Province)", *Journal of the Royal Anthropological Institute,* 60 (July–December 1930), pp. 283–334 was a preliminary study for the larger work. (Ed.)

# INTRODUCTION

The people of the Dukku tribe are virtually unknown outside the immediate area of the border of Yauri and Kontagora Emirates in the North Western State of Nigeria.[1] The few brief articles that have been written about them have little practical value for modern scholars interested in this tribe. None of them are recent. One, which was published in 1920,[2] was used as a basis for the others which were published later. Much of the information presented might have been true fifty years ago, but certainly it has only limited relevance today — and, indeed, is even misleading. There are moreover, certain claims made in it which research has not been able to substantiate as having ever existed (e. g. that the Dukku and Kamberi languages are mutually intelligible).[3] Repeated mis-information of such a nature does more harm than good. Also, from the material contained in these articles, one must doubt whether any of the authors spent any length of time living among the Dukku people.

I was encouraged to accumulate the information contained in the following pages for several reasons.

1.  The general lack of information about the Dukkawa. I spent over nine years living among these people; living and sleeping in their compounds, eating their food, attending their feasts, and generally observing their manner of life.

---

[1]     Virtually the only serious attempt to describe the Dukkawa began and ended with Temple (O and C.L.), *Notes on the Tribes, Provinces, Emirates and States of the Northern Provinces of Nigeria;* C.M.S., Lagos, 1919, pp. 96-100. This work was republished in 1965 by F. Cass & Co. Ltd., London. *(Ed.)*

[2]     Actually in 1919, the Temple work. *(Ed.)*

[3]     *Ibid. (Ed.)*

2. Even to this day, the tribe has been singularly free from outside influences. The people are scattered throughout the bush and seldom intermingle with other tribes except on market days. As such, they offer a remarkable opportunity for the observation of their autonomous development "from within".

3. Many of these people are my friends and I have never regarded them merely as objects of a survey. As a result of our mutual relationship, therefore, I have been able to obtain information which might have been difficult, or even impossible, for an "outsider".

4. Finally — and this is the most important aspect if this book is to have any value — I have bound myself to write only about those things which I have personally experienced and can verify.

In some cases where added explanations have been required, my years of living among the Dukkawa have enabled me to obtain them from reliable and trustworthy informants. I have, however, always rechecked such "added" information with many Dukkawa from various sections of the tribal area, and whenever there has been a lack of agreement on any particular point, I have omitted all reference to it. Although a few minor points may thereby have been left out, the reader can be certain that everything contained herein does exist here and now.

The Dukkawa of Northwest Nigeria

# MAP OF THE YELWA AREA

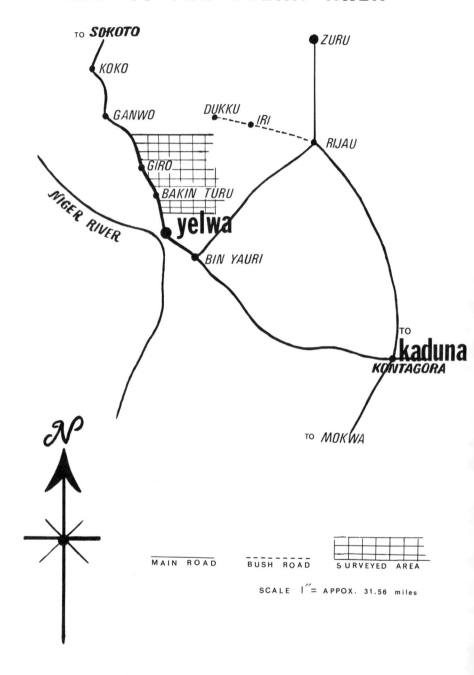

TO **SOKOTO**

ZURU

KOKO

GANWO

DUKKU

IRI

RIJAU

GIRO

BAKIN TURU

NIGER RIVER

yelwa

BIN YAURI

TO
**kaduna**
**KONTAGORA**

TO MOKWA

N

MAIN ROAD          BUSH ROAD          SURVEYED AREA

SCALE  1" = APPOX. 31.56 miles

Sketch Map of the Yelwa (Yauri) Area of the Sokoto Province of the Northwest State of Nigeria, Showing the Location of the Area Surveyed by the Author in the Following Chapters.

## CHAPTER I

# LOCATION AND ENVIRONMENT

## GENERAL SITUATION

The town of Yelwa (Yauri), in the North Western State of Nigeria, is located on the eastern bank of the Niger River. At 11° N latitude − 4° 50′ W longitude, it is 360 miles north-northeast of Lagos; 200 miles west of Kaduna; and 160 miles south-southeast of Sokoto.

More precisely, Yelwa can be described in relation to the following towns in its general area:

Kontagora is 65 miles to the southeast; Koko is 50 miles to the north; Rijau is 45 miles to the east; and Zuru is 70 miles to the northeast, (all measured by road). The area which forms the Dukku tribal-land begins about eight miles north of Yelwa, on the road to Sokoto, near a settlement called Golongo and continues northward for about twenty miles. There are no Dukkawa living in any of the towns along this stretch of road, and except for a few compounds immediately to the west of it, the main location penetrates some six or seven miles eastward from this road into the bush.

The following excerpt from a previous study of the people is still applicable:

> The only breakdown of Dukkawa is on a predominantly geographical, and to some extent political basis, by which the main body of Dukkawa are shown to be located in the western and northern part of Rijau District. . ; a much smaller group in the eastern part of the same district. . ; and one still smaller, to the west, in the *Shanga District of Yauri Emirate.*[1]

---

[1] See H.D. Gunn and F.P. Conant, *Peoples of the Middle Niger Region − Northern Nigeria;* I.A.I., London, 1960, pp. 49−50.

It is precisely in this last-mentioned Shanga District that the Dukka who come under the present survey are located.

In reference to the above excerpt, the description of the "main body of Dukkawa" corresponds with what the Dukkawa themselves assert, although the present case study does not involve itself with the Rijau area. However, the reference does not appear appropriately to describe the full extent of the Dukkawa's habitation, especially to the north and south of Yelwa. Dukku settlements are known to exist near Koko — fifty miles north of Yelwa, and within ten miles of Kontagora — which is sixty-five miles southeast. In both instances, the Dukkawa claim to live in the immediate areas (although a personal visit was not made to their compounds). There are no statistics as to the number of Dukkawa at these two extremities but, even so, it would appear that Dukkawa habitation is now more extensive than was the case when previous studies were compiled.[2]

## TRIBAL SUBDIVISIONS.

The Dukkawa who form the present sample have emigrated westward from two general areas. The majority of them (or their parents or grandparents) came from the area around Dukku; the balance came from the area around Iri. These are the only two subdivisions within the tribe, and the Dukkawa themselves readily provided information concerning other groups located in the Rijau and Zuru areas.

The groups concerned are: Shingiri, Upawki, Udu, Doge, Cenjiri, Kirhaw, Katagiwa, Abka, Dirin Daji, and Makuku.

The Dukku herein described, as stated, all trace their background to either Dukku or Iri, but before discussing the people themselves, it is well first to characterize the environment in which they live.

---

[2] This is undoubtedly the case for many similar groups also. It was an inevitable outcome of the *Pax Britannica*. The most spectacular example is that of the Tiv, a tribe which began its migration before the Colonial era, but whose spread many hundreds of miles from its homeland can only have been facilitated by it. *(Ed.)*

## TOPOGRAPHY.

The elevation of the Shanga District is between five and six hundred feet. As previously noted, the sample area begins about eight miles north of Yelwa and the Niger, which branches northwest from Yelwa so that the river has no practical or economic significance for the Dukkawa.

The terrain is generally flat, but contains extensive areas of gradually rolling and sloping ground, and is typical of the prevailing orchard bush common to the north of Nigeria. From any given point an observer can usually see at least a mile in any direction, and often much further (except, of course, during the farming season when the many fields of ten-foot high guineacorn[3] obstruct the view). With the exception of scattered baobab trees,[4] which average about forty feet in height, few trees are more than twenty feet high. The scene is in marked contrast both to the man-made wide-open spaces to be seen in the north around Sokoto or Kano and the thicker and more densely foliaged rainforests which are found two hundred and fifty miles to the south.

The land occasionally rises into low hill formations, tapering off into wide valley-like expanses, causing shallow ravines where the water runs off during the rainy season. Due to the rocky composition of the land, these ravines seldom exceed four or five feet in depth and are very irregular in their courses, washing out the more sandy sections.

In general, the soil itself is sandy and coarse. Consequently it is highly permeable and has a low water-retention capacity. It is typically lateritic, well leached, and lacking in organic matter.

---

[3] *Sorghum Vulgare*, some twenty varieties of which are recognised and named in Hausa. *(Ed.)*

[4] *Adansonia Digitata*, also sometimes called the Monkey Bread Tree. The leaves, said to be exceptionally high in vitamin A, are a frequent addition to soups and sauces, while its fruit-pods provide an acid, pleasantly "chewy", pulp often used in food and drinks. The fiber from the bark is used to make ropes, twine and especially fiddle strings. *(Ed.)*

CLIMATE

The principal seasonal variations of climate can be classified as follows: —

The Harmattan: (Hausa: *Buda*) That time of year when the air is clouded with dust-like sand particles which are blown southward from the Sahara Desert. It is familiar to all who have traveled in many parts of West Africa.

The season usually begins in late October or November and continues into late February or early March. There is frequently considerable variation from year to year. For example, in 1969 the Harmattan season began late in December and continued intermittently until as late as mid-April. On a particularly 'heavy' Harmattan day, visibility is reduced to two or three hundred yards and, it is possible even at noonday to look at the sun and observe it as a perfect sphere, much as through a smoked glass.

The Hot Season: (Hausa: *Rani*) begins in late February and by mid-March has reached its full, which will continue until some time in May when the temperature will begin to diminish.[5] These months of March-April-May are the hottest time of the year. During the first two of these months, the temperature almost always exceeds one hundred degrees, and May's slight decrease in temperature is counter-balanced by a considerable increase in humidity. The foliage disappears almost completely and the general appearance of the terrain is gradually transformed, into a bleak, burnt-out brown. The lateritic soil hardens into a cement-like surface and hope for the renewal of vegetation seem non-existent.

*Bazara;* is the Hausa name (there is no English equivalent) for the transitional period which occurs about mid-May when the Hot Season begins to diminish in intensity and signs of the coming rainy season become more apparent. Such signs consist of increasing cloudiness and occasional electric storms which frequently result more in dust-swirling than actual rainfall.

The Rainy Season: (Hausa: *Damuna*) usually begins in late May and lasts through mid-October. The months of July-August-

---

[5] This same season is sometimes called the "Dry Season", but this can be misleading. Actually, it is "dry" from mid-October until the following May in the normal course of events.

September are the height of the rains, after which they will then diminish very quickly in early October, so that by the latter part of that month they usually finish entirely.

As the rains cease the Harmattan again begins to make its appearance, thus completing the yearly cycle.


TEMPERATURE AND HUMIDITY.


Since both temperature and humidity exert a very definite influence on levels of activity, it was felt to be worth recording a yearly sample. The following statistics for the Yelwa area were obtained from the Nigerian Meterology Office. They relate to the monthly averages over a ten year period — from 1950 to 1959 — and pertain to maximum temperature, minimum temperature, maximum humidity, and minimum humidity. The average amount of monthly rainfall during this period is also noted.[6]

| Month | Max. Temp. | Min. Temp. | Max. Hum. | Min. Hum. | Rain in inches. |
|-------|-----------|-----------|-----------|-----------|-----------------|
| Jan.  | 96.3  | 59.5 | 58.5% | 15.9% | 8.02  |
| Feb.  | 99.5  | 64.7 | 49.3  | 15.7  | 0.16  |
| Mar.  | 102.4 | 73.9 | 56.6  | 22.0  | 0.29  |
| April | 100.9 | 78.3 | 67.3  | 30.7  | 0.60  |
| May   | 95.1  | 76.6 | 82.0  | 48.6  | 5.11  |
| June  | 90.5  | 73.8 | 88.5  | 57.5  | 4.74  |
| July  | 86.5  | 72.1 | 92.8  | 67.0  | 9.19  |
| Aug.  | 85.3  | 72.0 | 94.4  | 71.0  | 8.53  |
| Sep.  | 87.7  | 71.2 | 95.3  | 67.0  | 9.44  |
| Oct.  | 90.9  | 70.4 | 94.9  | 56.4  | 3.45  |
| Nov.  | 96.9  | 62.7 | 90.9  | 28.5  | 0.001 |
| Dec.  | 96.1  | 56.7 | 75.4  | 18.7  | 0.002 |

---

[6] Measurements in °F. in respect of temperatures. *(Ed.)*

Several pertinent observations arise from these statistics.

(A)  From October to June — a period of nine consecutive months — the maximum daily temperature averages more than 90° reaching a peak during the months of March and April when the maximum temperature averages more than 100°.

(B)  The three months of the year when the maximum temperature does not average 90° — i.e. July, August and September — are part of the most humid time of the year when the maximum daily humidity is always over 90% and the minimum humidity never gets even as low as 65%.

(C)  The greatest temperature fluctuation occurs during the month of December when there is a daily variation of forty degrees from the heat of the day to the cool of the morning hours. (This is quite a noticeable contrast to months like July, August, and September when there is seldom a temperature variation of more than fifteen degrees during any twenty four hour period.) This severe daily fluctuation in December's temperatures becomes significant when it is remembered that most cases of pneumonia and other respiratory diseases occur around this time of year from November to February.

In summary, while the climate in this area cannot be said to be unbearable, it is certainly far from ideal! The high temperatures and high humidity have a distinctly enervating effect which is reflected in the levels of activity of the people.

It might be claimed that this information as to land and climate has been presented in too much detail. However, it affects so many aspects of Dukku life — water supply, times for feasts, hunting, etc. — that a very clear understanding of it is important for a full appreciation of much that follows.

## CHAPTER TWO

# PHYSICAL APPEARANCE

## A.   PHYSICAL CHARACTERISTICS

Of the various tribes which inhabit the Yelwa area, Hausa, Fulani, Gungawa, Sarkawa, Shangawa, Kamberi, and Dukkawa only the latter are characterized by *filed teeth* (Fig. 2). Occasionally a Kamberi will have his front two upper teeth filed, but certainly this is not  a common enough practice to be called characteristic of that tribe as a whole. On the other hand, the majority of Dukku men and women have at least some of their teeth filed.

This custom in not mandatory, although most Dukkawa do it, and it is done "as the person likes it." Usually it is only the upper teeth that are filed, but some — especially women — also have some of their bottom teeth filed also. It is, however, strictly a personal matter and there is no special significance in the number of teeth that are treated. Some file only the front two teeth, although usually more are shaped than that, sometimes four, sometimes as many as are visible when a person smiles. Though the teeth are said to be "filed", actually they are chipped to a sharp 'V' by being hammered with a chisel-like piece of metal, starting at the ridge and working toward the gum. The blacksmith usually performs this task which is very slow and painful, especially as the chipping approaches the gum. When a person wants to have many teeth worked on, they are usually done two by two, allowing several days for the finished teeth to heal before continuing work on the others.

There is no ceremony connected with this practice. It is merely a case of a person wanting to have it done, and of the blacksmith doing it. Nor is there any special age when it is felt that it should be done. One man related how, one evening, he returned

Fig. 2. A fine example of Dukku orthodontia! Chipped teeth in both upper and lower jaws. Note also the arm bands.

Fig. 3. Front view of an excellent example of Dukku cicatricing. The *kada* pattern is seen on the abdomen. Note also the arm bands, nose tack and hair style.

Fig. 4. Back view of same.

from his farm and found that his seven year old son had two of his teeth filed. On being asked if he had been angry with the boy, he replied that it was their custom and if the boy wanted to do it, it was all right with him. "They're his teeth!" he said.

It would doubtless be very dramatic if some cultural or superstitious reason could be adduced for this custom of chipped teeth one visitor, upon seeing a BaDukku for the first time, suggested they might formerly have been cannibals! But, unfortunately, none such can be provided. They do it because they think it looks nice, and this is surely the basic reason for "fashion" the world over. One elderly Dukku man told me that this custom had a practical value years ago when Dukkawa were having trouble with other tribes. Seeing a person with filed teeth, they would not mistakenly capture one of their own people. True or not, the custom does not have any practical or remembered value today.

As with many other tribes in Nigeria, the Dukkawa have distinctive *tribal markings*. With some tribes, the incisions are so severe that the healed scars result in serious alterations of facial contour, but with the Dukkawa the markings are made so fine and are so meticulously executed that the skin generally remains smooth. Besides the customary facial markings, almost any other part of the body can also be marked: neck, arms, chest, legs. Men never have markings on their back, but such are very popular with girls and women. Those who do the actual marking receive from one to ten shillings,[1] depending on how much of the body is marked (Figs. 3 and 4).

The process itself is very painful, a very sharp knife being used to incise the skin just deep enough to produce blood. Then charcoal, which has been pounded into a fine powder, is rubbed into the wound. Although the person can choose any kind of markings he desires, there are some general patterns. Some of these are:

1.  *k'ulik'uli*, a circular design named after small fried cakes;

2.  *kalangu*, named after a type of stringed drum;

3.  *kadangare* — lizard;

4.  *kibiya* — arrow;

5.  *aku* — parrot;

6.  *kada* — crocodile

These designs are not exact replicas of the items they purport to be, as in western society when a man would have a boat or bird tatooed on his chest or arm, but are patterns which stylistically represent the names given to them.

As with the filing of teeth, the patterns of the markings and how much of the body is to be marked is strictly a personal matter. However, most young children, before they are old enough to

---

[1] Throughout this study, the pre-1968 coinage is used. One shilling was then approximately the equivalent of 15¢ or a fraction less. The present Nigerian currency (*Naira* and *Kobo*) have not been used by the author. (Ed.)

make these choices, already have some facial markings. Children as young as six months old have been observed with facial markings. In these cases, it is ordinarily the mother of the child who decides to have it done and chooses the design.

In the ethnological survey *Peoples of the Middle Niger Region, Northern Nigeria*[2] I found the following statement:

> "Tribal marks are no longer a basis of identification; often they are omitted, or simply cut to individual taste. Temple describes Dukkawa tribal marks in former times as being sixteen parallel scoring on each cheek,[3] with another sixteen parallel short lines between eye and ear. . ."

With regard to the Dukkawa, however, the following observations would seem to be more accurate: —

1. *Marks not a basis of identification.* Since the designs are a matter of personal choice, it is true that there is no one characteristic mark(s) which bespeaks a BaDukku, in contrast to the system in many other tribes. On the other hand, the style of the markings — the very delicate and precise incisions, the effect of the rubbing of the charcoal into them — all clearly differentiate a BaDukku from a person of any other indigenous tribe in the Yelwa area. In this sense, therefore the process could be described as having a basis of identification.

2. *Marks often omitted.* Among approximately five hundred Dukkawa encountered on a day to day basis, *only one young teen-age boy was found who had absolutely no markings at all.*

3. *Marks in former times being sixteen parallel scorings on each cheek,* etc. This statement, in itself, is not in question since such considerable authorities as the Temples must be given full credit for observations made in their day. These sixteen scorings, however, are certainly not the case now, and, as far as can be seen, the present pat-

---

[2] Gunn and Conant; *op. cit.* p. 52.

[3] Temple, O & C.L.; *op. cit.* p. 96 (Ed.)

terns of Dukku markings give no indication as to how they might have evolved from such.[4]

It is worth noting, also, in reference to these sixteen parallel markings, that the description given roughly corresponds to the markings of some Shangawa and Sarkawa people in the Yelwa area. Although the number of scorings vary — from eight to thirteen — they are certainly parallel scorings on the sides of both cheeks.

## B.   CLOTHING.

Children begin wearing clothes at the age of four or five years. Older Dukkawa say that, when they were young, children did not wear clothes until eight or nine years of age. A boy's first loincloth is either made, or bought, by his father; a girl's first piece of cloth — used to wrap around her waist — is bought for her by her mother.

Loinclothes are made from thin-skinned animals such as sheep, goats, duiker, small gazelle, and monkeys. Sometimes the skin of a cat is used for a small boy's loincloth. If purchased in the marketplace, ram skin and she-goat skin loincloths are the most expensive, costing about ten shillings each. Types made from other skins cost seven or eight shillings. A boy's loincloth costs three shillings.

But, whenever possible, the Dukkawa make their own loin-cloths. The animal skin is soaked in cold water and then spread on the ground, hair down, to dry. It is covered on the fleshy side with cornstalk ash and then it is rolled up and left until the following day when the ashes are scraped off and the hair removed, after which the skin is treated with sheanut[5] oil and again left to dry.

---

[4] It should be pointed out, however, that the evolution or development of an existing practice or custom is not the only method of change. Sometimes a custom is dropped completely and a new one altogether is adopted. An example of this will be seen later in regard to the wearing of lip rings by women. Such a change may, therefore, well have occurred in respect to former and present-day patterns of cicatrice.

[5] Oil made from the nuts of the Butyrospermum Parkii (Hausa; *kad'anya*), the Shea Butter Tree. The fat (for it is scarcely "oil") from these nuts is used for cooking, as an illuminant, as the basis of unguents and as a dressing for leather.

Then follows a process called *ruwan toka*.[6] A large calabash is placed on the ground, and another smaller perforated, or cracked calabash is placed above it. Some grass is put in the smaller calabash, and then the grass is covered with cornstalk ashes. Cold water is poured over the ashes and filters through the grass and perforations into the larger calabash underneath until it is nearly filled. Then the seeds of a small fruit melon are mixed into the *ruwan toka*. The animal skin is then placed in this water and left to soak thoroughly for two days, after which it is removed to dry, is stretched, and, again treated with sheanut oil for softness. Finally, it is cut to shape for wear, being slit to be tied around the waist, with the main length of the skin hanging down the back, to be brought between the legs and then lapped over in front.

Some tribes, such as the Kamberi, sometimes decorate their loinclothes with cowry beads or other ornamentation, but this is not customary among the Dukkawa.

This leather loincloth is the Dukku man's usual clothing whenever at home or on his farm. Even when going to market he might wear it — unless he has a pair of short pants (which cost between four and ten shillings) — but on such an occasion he will also wrap a colored piece of cloth across his shoulders, or wear a long jumper-type shirt which falls down across the hips.

The wrapper cloth referred to above is worn in a slightly different manner by Dukku men from that of some of the other local tribes. It is draped over one shoulder and under the other, with the ends being tied in front.

The cloth hangs down to just above the knees. Some Gungawa have been seen to wrap the cloth around their backs, cross it in front under their arms, and then bring the two ends behind their necks to be tied. The Dukkawa have not been observed wearing their cloth in this manner. Other groups will often just take the cloth and fold it over their shoulders, the end hanging down the back, without tying it at all.

The piece of cloth which Dukku men use as a wrapper across their shoulder is almost always a patterned design chosen according to personal taste. There is no characteristically "Dukkawa pat-

---

[6] Literally "Ash water".

tern," nor is there any certain color for this cloth which could be called typical of the Dukkawa.[7]

Rubber 'sandals,' made from discarded motor tires, are the common modern type of foot wear. These cost about one shilling and six pence. At home, a BaDukku — both men and women — will either wear these tire-sandals, or just go barefoot, but some kind of footwear will usually be worn when leaving the compound. Imported rubber (proper) sandals and rubber imitation shoes will be worn by those who can afford them — about ten shillings — for special occasions and, sometimes, when going to market.

Women's apparel is very simple. It consists of a piece of cloth — about five feet long and three feet wide — which is wrapped a-round the waist and either tucked in or held in place by a thin piece of cloth which is tied around the waist in belt-fashion and knotted in front. This cloth which women wrap around their waist should not be confused with the wrapper cloth Dukku men use across their shoulders. The women's cloth can be said to be typi-cally Dukku from two points of view: color and pattern. From a distance it appears to be a piece of solid dark blue cloth, but there are lines of red and white in the pattern. Almost every Dukku woman has a piece of cloth of this kind, exact in color and design. At home she will wear an older cloth of this kind; a newer or bet-ter one when going to market. Two yards of the cloth just de-scribed costs about twenty-five shillings.

Dukku women seldom cover their breasts, even when going to market or at special gatherings, unless it is the cool Harmattan Season or if they are carrying a baby on their back.

Sometimes a woman will wear an underskirt, *fatari*,[8] which is a narrower piece of cloth attached by strings. It is worn next to

---

[7] As, for example, blue can be said to predominate among the Yoruba, or white among the Hausa.

[8] The *fatari* is the women's loincloth. It could be translated either as "bloomers" or as "panties", for though a highly proper, decent and modest garment, Hausa slang (which is neither more nor less reflective of the practice than is that of other cultures) has endowed the word (and the garment) with a certain lubricity and a number of risqué synonyms, of which some of the more decent are *Sarkin Fada* — "Keeper of the Palace"; *Gagara Shari'a* — "One short step from a Lawsuit!"; *Tsamiyar Raba* — "The Silky Tease" and so on. (*Ed.*)

the body and the larger cloth is wrapped over it. At other times, just the large piece of cloth is worn.

When carrying a baby on the back, another piece of cloth is used. The baby is cradled in this, as in a sling, resting over the mother's buttocks, and the cloth is wrapped around and tucked in front, usually over the breasts.

When going to market, or on special occasions, some Dukka-wa women wear a head-scarf, but these are rather expensive and not too many women have them.

## C.   ORNAMENTATION.

Several times thus far reference has been made to 'feasts' and 'special gatherings.' Since reference to them will recurr, it will be simpler to describe them by the Hausa word *biki*. The various kinds of *biki* will be considered in a later chapter, but for now a general description will suffice. Basically, a biki is a social event when Dukkawa — men, women, children, — gather together for one or more days of dancing, singing, and drinking. On such occasions special ornamentation is assumed.

*a. Facial markings.*

There is a cosmetic made from the shrub *gaude*[9] a preparation of the fruit of which produces a very black substance that is applied to the face with a pen-like instrument to make line designs. This can be done on the nose, forehead, cheeks and chin. This cosmetic temporarily stains the skin and cannot be washed off immediately.[10] Dukku girls and women will always use this cosmetic when going to a *biki,* and sometimes when going to market. Teen-age Dukku boys might also use it when going to a *biki* (Fig. 5).

*b. Headbands.*

Dukku women will frequently wear a thin leather (it looks like rubber, but is not) headband across their forehead. Some

---

[9] *Gardenia erubescens.* The cosmetic referred to is called *katambiri. (Ed.)*

[10] One European visitor learned this the hard way! While attending a Dukku *biki,* in a spirit of friendliness he consented to be marked in this manner. To his acute embarrassment, when he returned to his job, he found that he could not remove the marks.

women wear them all the time, others wear them just on certain occasions. The ornament merely consists of a thin piece of leather which is tied at the back of the head.

A fancier kind of headband, wider and with many small beads sewn into it, will be worn by girls and young unmarried women for *biki*. The beads can be any color but combinations of red and yellow are the most common. — Dukku men seldom wear any kind of a headband (Fig. 5).

### c. *Earrings.*

Unlike Kamberi men, Dukku men do not have pierced ears, nor do they wear any kind of ornamentation in their ears.

Most Dukku women have pierced ears and will wear earrings when going to market or to a *biki*. Some women will even wear a cheaper kind of earring — six pence to one shilling — when they are working around the compound.

The piercing of the ear is done by first warming the ear, then piercing it with a very sharp metal skewer.

### d. *Nose tacks.*

One very characteristic sign of Dukku women (not the men) is the wearing a tack — like a drawing pin or thumb tack — in one side of the nose, usually the left. No special piercing is done for this: if a girl is wearing one for the first time, she just slowly works it through the side of her nostril. Almost all Dukku women have a pierced nostril. These tacks, gold or silver in color, are either made by a blacksmith or are bought in the market for a few pennies. Although a woman from another tribe is occasionally seen with a nose tack, it is certainly not characteristic of any other tribe in the Yelwa area except the Dukkawa.

These nose tacks are a recent custom. Older Dukkawa say that when they were young they cannot recall Dukku women wearing them. The custom has replaced that of the women wearing lip-rings (Fig. 6).

### e. *Lip-rings.*

This form of ornament is definitely now becoming a thing of the past, at least in the area being considered. Occasionally an elderly Dukku woman is met who still wears these metal rings in her lips, but it is now not often found among young or middle-aged women. Some women wore rings in both upper and lower lips, others wore them just in the upper lip. A hole was pierced in the center of the lip with a hot piece of metal, then a piece of straw or thick grass was inserted into the hole, so as to prevent it from closing, and left there until healed. Then a bit of shiny wire or thin metal, formed in a ring, was inserted through the hole. As time went on, the hole gradually broadened and, when it was large enough, another ring was fitted. This might be repeated four or five times depending on the ability of the lip tissue to support the weight (Fig. 6).

*f. Eyes.*

There is a kind of galena,[11] — a natural lead sulphide — which the Dukkawa, both men and women use to adorn their eyes. It is carried in a small container together with a needlelike piece of metal for application. The needle is dipped in the galena and then placed against the eye — actually touching the cornea. The eyelid is closed over it and the needle is pulled through to the side. Some people use this merely for adornment, but many claim that the galena has medicinal value for eye strain and even temporary blindness.[12]

*g. Neck wear.*

Dukku men and women are fond of wearing neck cords or chains. Sometimes it is a proper silver chain which costs two or three shillings; other times a string of small beads, a cord, or thick string with a medal attached will serve. A favorite is the Maria Theresa dollar — rather bigger than a U. S. half-dollar piece — which Dukku women commonly wear (Fig. 3).

For *biki,* many teen-age girls and some young men, wear a special neck-band with many small beads sewn into it similar in craftmanship to the headbands mentioned above.

*h. Arm bands.*

These are worn just above the elbow. Almost all Dukku women wear strands of rubber — which cost about nine

---

[11] Hausa *kwalli* or *tozali.* This would appear to be antimony. The applicator is called *mishi.* See Fig. 7.

[12] The use of galena is not peculiar to the Dukkawa. It is commonly used in a great many parts of Africa. (Ed.)

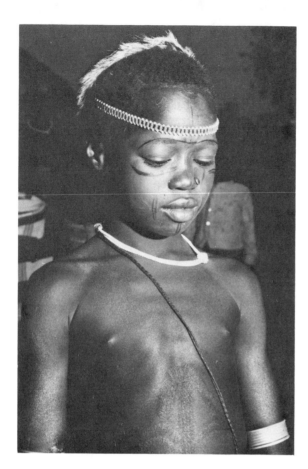

Fig. 5. Small girl made up for party. Note the thumbtack in the nose and the decorated headband.

Fig. 6. Dukku woman wearing lip rings. Though the custom is waning, this subject is not yet of middle age.

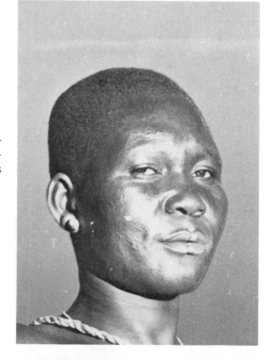

Fig. 7. Applying galena (antimony) to the eyes. The *kwalli* or *tozali* is kept in the hide bottle *(kuratandu)* and the cosmetic is applied with the *mishi* which in this case is held in the right hand.

pence a strand — wrapped around their arms. There is no special significance to the number of times it is wrapped around their arm it is just wrapped until no more is left. These bands are left on all the time, unless, as in the case of a growing girl, one becomes too tight and has to be replaced with another. When they are removed, there are callous marks on the arm caused by the constriction. For *biki,* girls and young women might wear special armbands with sewn-in beads as mentioned above (Fig. 2).

Some Dukku men might wear a single strand of rubber a-round their arm (but not wrapped around several times as the women do). Others occasionally put on an armband made from the skin of a goat or duiker, or wear a simple silver bracelet pushed up above the elbow.

There are also two special kinds of armbands which Dukkawa men wear.[13] As will be pointed out in a later chapter, Duk-kawa men are very good hunters, — as a group, the best a-mong the tribes in the area. Both of the armbands in question are made from the skin of the roan antelope, a large animal which is not too often killed.[14]

The first type consists of a narrow piece of skin, about half an inch in width, which has been treated with sheanut oil. The length is cut so that it is just long enough to be wrapped once a-round the upper arm. Holes are punched in both ends and a thin piece of leather is strung through them to fasten the band. On this type of band, the hair is left on.

The other type is made from a piece of dried roan antelope skin which is about six inches square — not a strip of skin, as in the former case. A sharp stick is used to pry a hole in the center of this skin, and the opening is worked wider and wider until it is large enough for the arm to pass through. Then the hair is removed — unlike the former type — with a knife, and the band is softened with sheanut oil and left to dry.

Since the roan antelope is one of the biggest animals to be found in the neighborhood — although the nearest area to the Dukkawa where they can be found today is about forty miles to the west — it may be suspected that armbands made from this skin convey a recognition of the Dukku prowess in hunting. If there is this tribal significance, rather than merely a sign of personal a-chievement, such a fact would explain why these bands may be worn by young and older males alike even those who have never themselves killed a roan antelope. These two armbands mentioned

---

[13] Not "special" in the sense of being elaborate or expensive, or even being in-tended as marks of distinction, but in the sense that the men themselves consider them to be part of their tradition.

[14] Hippotragus equinum gambianus (Hausa: *gwanki*). (Ed.)

above, however, are not worn by all the Dukku men, nor all the time by those who do wear them. One occasion when they would be worn would be when going to market, another when attending a *biki.*

### i. Rings

Rings are very common among Dukkawa, both men and women. They are merely for decoration and have no particular significance. As many as four or five rings can be worn on any finger of either hand, even the thumb, and they can be worn on several fingers. The most seen in wear were on the hands of a teen-age girl: she had four each on three fingers of one hand, and two on the small finger of the other hand. Some Dukkawa do not wear any rings, but most of them wear at least one. The rings themselves are simple metal objects, sometimes slightly twisted, which are easily made by the local blacksmiths.

### j. Henna.

This red dye is commonly used in many parts of Nigeria for staining the hands to a deep crimson color which is considered very beautiful. The henna is put into a long tube-shaped gourd and the hand is placed inside the gourd for about an hour. Then the hand is removed and wiped clean, producing the desired effect.

### k. Calf bands.

These are ordinarily worn only by girls and women. The common type is two or three strands of ordinary rubber (a little thicker then the rubber strands used to wrap around the arms) which are wound around the calf of the leg. Sometimes on both. For *biki,* a band with sewn-in colored beads (as described above) might also be tied around the calf instead of the plain ones.

### l. Cowry beads.

A specifically Dukku trait for women is wearing one strand of cowry beads around one, or both *ankles.* This has been the custom as long as anyone can now remember. Some Dukku women wear them all the time, others just on certain occasions — but all the women have them. Cowry beads are still very common in Nigeria — in pre-colonial times they were used in place of money — and are used extensively now by very many tribes for various kinds of ornamentation. For example, Kamberi men sew cowry beads on their travelling bags; Fulani women plait cowry beads in their hair; etc. But the particular custom of wearing them around the ankles seems to be peculiar to the Dukku woman (Fig. 8).

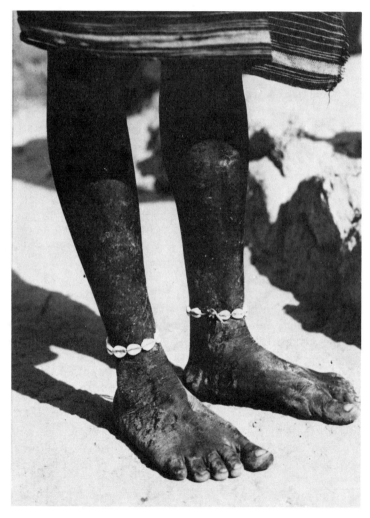

Fig. 8. Woman wearing cowry anklets. A peculiarly Dukku custom.

Occasionally a woman will be seen wearing a strand of cowry beads around her *neck*. Some people claim that this is in rememberance of someone who has died; most say it is merely a decoration with no special significance.

On rare occasions Dukku girls or women have been seen with a cowry bead bracelet on the *wrist*. One informant claimed that this is worn as a protection against the spirit of a deceased relative who is said to have revisited the family: the cowry bead bracelet is supposed to prevent the spirit from coming near the wearer. Even though only one informant produced this explanation, it has been included because it was not contradicted by other Dukkawa, who when asked, simply did not want to talk about it.

## CHAPTER THREE

# COMMUNITY LIVING

## A. THE SETTLEMENT.

There are three distinct characteristics of the Dukku life style.

1.  The Dukkawa do not live in towns, or even in small villages. They live in the bush itself.
2.  They live in distinct and separate compounds.
3.  These individual compounds are based on family relationship.

To find a compound, one must move off the main road and go into the bush. Golongo, Bakin Turu, Giro, and Ganwo are all villages or hamlets on the road north of Yelwa — eight, fourteen, twenty, and thirty miles from Yelwa respectively — in the immediate vicinity of which Dukkawa reside. But there are no Dukkawa living in any of these villages themselves.[1]

Dukku compounds are always small and well separated one from another, a fact which bespeaks a clear preference for privacy. There even seems to be a pattern in the way the compounds are

---

[1] The Dukkawa afford a classic example of a "Granary Civilization" within the terms of Maquet's analysis. See Maquet J. *Les Civilizations Noires,* Horizons de France, Paris, 1962.

Indeed, the Northern States of Nigeria are rich in similar examples, both of the archtypical such as the Dukkawa represent, and the more technologically complex such as the Matakam and Gwoza of Sardauna Province and near Bokkos on the Plateau, where some excellent examples of the "Terraced Granary Civilization" (not described by Maquet) can be observed.

A good case could be argued that it was from the evolution of this latter pattern that impetus was provided for the technological mutation that gave rise to another of Maquet's classifications, the "Civilization of the Cities" so well exemplified in the "Walled Cities" which formed the fortress nuclei of the Hausa States. (*Ed.*)

separated. Usually a group of two or three compounds will be found within seventy-five to two hundred yards of one another, then another similar group a quarter or half mile away, and so on.

The basis for determining membership of a compound is that of immediate patrilineal relationship: a father, his sons and their families. If a man has several sons, some of them when married may move out of the father's compound and build their own, though at least one married son will always remain in the father's compound.

When an elderly man dies, sometimes some of the sons will break away from the main compound to set up house-keeping on their own. At other times they will all remain together.

Two examples of how this arrangment operates are:

1. In the first instance, the compound was a mile and a half off the main road into the bush. Two older brothers lived here with their families. About a quarter of a mile behind this compound there were three other compounds arranged in a rough triangle, about seventy-five yards apart from each other. In each of these compounds there was one married man and his family. A footpath led, after about another quarter of a mile, to a small compound where a young married man lived with his wife and child. Five hundred yards further on there were two more compounds about a hundred yards apart: in the first lived a man with one married son (and family) and one teen-age son; in the second, a twenty-five year old married man and his two younger brothers. Almost half a mile further on was a large compound where an elderly man lived with his five married and three unmarried sons. This particular compound, with seventeen adults in it, was one of the three largest compounds in the vicinity. This pattern was repeated throughout the immediate community.

2. The settlement was about ten miles from the one previously described. The first compound was only about three hundred yards off the main road, although it was almost completely secluded from passers-by, being sighted

in a slight depression in the land and with a grove of small trees surrounding it.

The compound was larger than that of the average for the Dukkawa. Four married brothers lived there with their families and two unmarried brothers — eleven adults altogether. A quarter mile to the north there were four more compounds within a radius of five hundred yards. One of these housed two brothers and their families; the other three each consisted of one married man and his family. Eastward, back in the bush, and almost a mile away lay the next three compounds: one with an old man and two married sons, another with an old man and one married son, and the third consisting of two brothers and their families. These three compounds were all within one hundred yards of each other.

Description of a Typical Compound.

Almost invariably, a Dukku compound is enclosed within a fence. Where there is no fence, it probably means that the old one has been taken down and a new one has not yet been put up, although there are a few compounds that have been observed which have never been known to have been fenced at all.

There are two kinds of fences, the most common being made of cornstalks. Space is left for either one or two entrances, depending on the size and situation of the compound. For this kind of fence, straight wooden poles are set in the ground two or three feet apart all around the compound. They are usually about two inches in diameter and stand about six or six and a half feet high. Cornstalks are then laid on the ground and laced to the uprights by means of a grass or hemp rope. More cornstalks are added and laced, and so on until the fence reaches a height of about six feet.

The second kind of fence, which is much less common and only used around very small compounds or for certain sections of a compound as a partition, is made from trees about six or eight inches in diameter. The logs are sunk into the ground next to each other around the entire compound, or in that section of the compound to be partitioned. They are stabilized by two horizontal strands of cornstalks, at about two and four feet from the ground. For each strand, there are four or five cornstalks on one side, and the same number on the other side and at the same level. A rope is then run between each of the logs, tightly binding the cornstalks on both sides together, and thus securing the log between them.

## B.   ARCHITECTURE

The four primary constructions in any compound are:

1.   A granary (for storage of guinea corn) — (Hausa: *rumbu*)
2.   A personal hut — (Hausa: *d'aki*)
3.   A guest hut (Hausa: *zaure*)
4.   A kitchen (Hausa: *madafa*)

When starting to build a new compound, the granary and the personal hut are the first two buildings to be constructed. Storage of food and living quarters are of first importance, later on, if needs be, a hut can be built for visitors. The kitchen is the last to be constructed since there is no immediate urgency for it.

Building new huts, or repairing old ones, always takes place after the harvesting is finished and the men have been released from the full-time pressures of farming. This is usually in January or February when the last rains are two or three months past, and when the women do all of their cooking outside, so that the construction of the kitchen can be delayed somewhat.

Besides these four primary huts, there are others which are eventually built. Women usually have a storage bin — *rumbun mata* —[2] for their personal belongings, cooking utensils, storing left-over food etc. Ordinarily every married woman has her own *rumbun mata*. If a man has two wives, each wife will have a separate storage bin and unmarried girls would usually share one together.

Some women will have a small granary for storing guinea corn which is given to them or which they themselves buy for making guinea corn beer, which is the only alcoholic beverage drunk by the Dúkkawa.

---

[2] Though *rumbu* is usually translated merely as "cornbin", it has in fact a generic meaning as "store" or "storage place", even "attic" in the common English usage. Thus *rumbun mata* really means "woman's storage place", or even "pantry". *(Ed.)*

If there are one or more children in the family, when they reach the age of about ten, a separate hut is built for them; until that age they sleep with the parents. A separate hut is constructed for the girls, another for the boys.

There may, on occasion, also be special huts for the domestic animals, chickens, she-goats, etc.

Construction of Huts.

Living huts, in common with most other constructions, are made from mud, mixed with grass for strength, and they have thatched grass roofs. The exception to this rule is the granary which is of completely mud construction and only has a thatch cap over the upper part for additional protection against the rain. Soil from termite hills is always favored for building.

There are two ways of building with mud. The more common, and stronger type of construction is called *jan gini*.[3] When the mudgrass mixture has been prepared, a large handful is scooped out and placed on the ground where the base of the wall will be. The mud is then worked back and fourth between the hands — spreading it as far as it will extend — to a thickness of about three inches and a height of eight inches (it will not set firmly if built higher than this). This process is continued in circular fashion — virtually all Dukku huts are circular in shape — until the entire base of the wall is formed. One eight-inch layer is laid down in the morning, allowed to dry for half a day, and another eight-inch layer is added in the evening. This is continued on the next day and subsequently, until the wall is finished. At this rate, without interruptions, construction of a wall takes nine or ten days.

Another method of building the wall is by using mud blocks. The mud is formed into blocks about eighteen inches long and six inches high. The blocks are set in place before they dry and are then hand-moulded into position. Several layers of blocks are laid, up to two feet high, before they are left to dry. The next day

---

[3] This phrase, which literally means "pulling or dragging in the process of construction in mud" is extremely difficult to translate. It may best be rendered as "The Consolidated Method", or even (almost) "The Continuous Pouring Method", as opposed to *tubali* (sun dried brick) construction. The name originates because the material is "drawn" into a continuous form at each level of the process. *(Ed.)*

several more layers are added. Using these blocks a wall can be constructed in four or five days. This type of building is not as strong as *jan gini* because the blocks do not set as firmly as the mud which is built up.

Unless there is a necessity to build a hut quickly, or it is only intended for temporary use, the Dukkawa will always use the method of *jan gini*.[4]

As far as the style in which the various buildings are constructed is concerned, basically there are two constructions: the granary — having in mind its purpose — is made in one way; the other main huts personal hut, guest hut, and kitchen are generally built in another. So it will suffice to describe the granary and the personal hut — *d'aki,* — merely pointing out any ways in which either the guest hut or kitchen may vary in construction from a *d'aki*.

Construction of a Granary.

This is a unique building for several reasons. First, as pointed out above, it is the only construction which is entirely built from mud. All the other huts have mud walls, on top of which sticks are placed to which a thatched grass roof is attached. Second, the granary is usually the largest building in the compound. Third, any of the other huts can be constructed by *jan gini* or from mud blocks, but the granary is always built by *jan gini*.[5]

As mentioned above, *jan gini* is a stronger type of construction than that of blocks, so both from the point of view of added protection for the grain that will be stored inside, as well as the need for extra support for this large building, and especially for the mud roof, *jan gini* is necessary.

---

[4] It must be seriously questioned whether the "block method" is traditional to the Dukkawa, or whether it represents a technological borrowing. The oblong nature of the blocks bear a striking resemblance to the "Landcrete" blocks which were greatly encouraged by the Colonial Government in the years immediately following the Second World War. Oblong blocks are not usual in traditional building methods. Hausa builders, who do use "bricks" in massive constructions made of mud, make them pear-shaped. Another (more positive) example of Dukku ability to adopt new technologies will be referred to later. (*Ed.*)

[5] Which would seem to reinforce the argument advanced in 4 above. (*Ed.*)

When building a granary, the first thing that is done is to place large flat stones, standing upright, around the circumference which will form the base of the wall. These stones stand ten to twelve inches out of the ground. Then the same kind of stones are placed about one foot apart within the entire circumference. Sticks are then placed on top of these stones, joining them altogether, after which the first layer of mud is spread on top of the sticks.

This means that there is a space of ten to twelve inches between the ground and the floor of the granary. This elevated floor is necessary to prevent rain, or, indeed, moisture of any kind from seeping in at the base of the wall and spoiling the guinea corn which is inside.

Figure 9 shows an example of the base construction: stones interspaced a foot apart, on top of which sticks are used to link them to one another, providing a surface on which the mud floor can be laid.

After the first layer of the mud dries, a second layer is put down, making a total floor thickness of six to eight inches. Then the floor is hand-polished for smoothness.

After the floor is finished, or while the final layer is drying, the wall is begun. It is thicker at the base (about four inches) and tapers to about a three-inch thickness at the top. Some granary walls are built straight upward, others belly out slightly (Fig. 10).

At a height of about six feet, the wall is thickened about two inches to form a ledge around the entire top of the wall. Every twelve or fifteen inches along this ledge, two holes an inch apart are punched through with thin pieces of cornstalk. These cornstalks remain in position until the mud dries, then they are removed leaving small, well-formed holes. Later, when the structure is complete, a piece of hemp rope will be laced through these holes and through the first layer of thatching grass that will cover the roof.

Above the ledge, the mud construction continues upward, at first bulging outward slightly and then rounding over towards the top until only an opening of two and a half or three feet remains. The circumference of this opening is thickened and built up about from four to six inches, over which a cone shaped grass "hatch"

Fig. 9. Rock and pole base on which a granary will be built.

Fig. 10. A granary, before thatching.

will be made to fit securely. Since the granary has solid walls around, this opening at the top is the only method of entry.

To enter, a heavy pronged pole is leant against the side of the granary, the pronged end resting on the roof for stability. The person wishing to enter climbs up this rough ladder to the opening, removes the grass "hatch" and lowers himself down inside the granary (Fig. 11).

When the mud building is finished, a dry grass thatch is made up with hempen cord — *rama*.[6] The resultant "mat" is carefully measured so that it is long enough to reach the ledge to the entrance-opening at the top. The sewing is done about three inches from one end, and when enough grass has been sewn around the entire roof, it is rolled up on the ground, raised up to the roof, and unravelled around the ledge.

The hemp binding is immediately secured to the ropes that have been strung through the ledge holes. Towards the top of the bin, where it curves inward towards the entrance opening, the grass itself is interwoven to fit tightly against the roof. Finally, at the base of the entrance opening, the grass is braided together to form a knot (Fig. 12).

All that then remains is to make a grass covering which will fit securely over the entrance opening.

The size of a granary is determined solely by the number of people in the compound, i. e. how much guinea corn has to be stored for the year. Some of the biggest are about ten or eleven feet high.

Whenever there are several families living together in one compound, i. e. a man and his married sons, there will usually be one common granary for the compound, and then each son will have his own.

The hut in which women store their personal belongings — the *rumbun mata* — is constructed in a manner similar to a granary — hence the similarity in names! However, there are several basic differences.

For a *rumbun mata* five or six large stones are placed in a circle at the base, with one stone in the center. Since the base of

---

[6] *Hibiscus Cannabinus*, also known as Indian Hemp and Bastard Jute.

Fig. 11. Using the granary ladder.

Fig. 12. Putting bundles of
corn into the granary.

this hut is much smaller than the base of a granary the number of stones necessary within the circumference of the granary base for support is much reduced for the *rumbun mata.*

Moreover, whereas the stones at the base of a granary are covered with sticks, on top of which a level mud floor is laid, in this case the mud is built directly on top of the stones. It is constructed in such a way that it 'fans out' as it increases in height until it interjoins (Fig. 13).

The final difference is the siting of the entrance. A *rumbun mata* has a completely solid mud roof over which a thatch is put. The entrance is a hole, about one and a half feet square, which is cut into the ledge. To put articles inside, or to remove anything, a woman will stand on something to elevate herself so she can lean inside – she never enters completely (Fig. 14).

A *d'aki* has one doorway. Sometimes the door-frame is marked off at the beginning of construction by cornstalks tied in a ∏ form and the construction is built around this. Another way is to build the complete circular wall, and then chop out the door-way with an axe.

The thickness of the wall is two to three inches, and it reaches a height between five and a half and six feet. This is where the mud construction of a *d'aki* stops; as well as that of all the other types of huts – unlike the granary which has a mud roof. The roof framework is started by using four straight seven-foot building poles, each of which are forked at about six inches at one end.[7] The bottom ends of these four poles are placed on the top of the wall. The forked ends – at the higher extremity – lean inward above the center of the hut. These forked ends are then interlocked with each other but are not tied together as yet.

The bottom ends of the poles, which rest on the top of the wall, are then secured by packing mud around them. After the initial four poles are thus firmly set in place, others are added – about one foot apart – around the entire circumference of the wall. At the top they rest against the four interlocked poles; at the

---

[7] This is the absolutely indispensible *gofa*, the forked building pole without which little or nothing could be constructed. The natural Y of the fork permits beams etc. to be fastened in place with a degree of strength and rigidity that would otherwise be impossible. *(Ed.)*

Fig. 13. A woman's storage bin *(rumbun mata)*

Fig. 14. Putting things into a *rumbun mata.*

base they are mud-packed to the top of the wall just as the others were. When all these poles are in place, starting about twelve inches above the top of the wall, thin cornstalks are interlaced through them — under one, over another, under the next, etc. This will be done all the way around. Another twelve or fifteen inches above this, a second similar interlacing is done, and so on every twelve or fifteen inches until the top is reached. At the top, the point where the original four sticks are interlocked — against which also the rest of the sticks are resting — is firmly bound with hemp rope.

When the roof framework is finished, the sewn mats of roofing grass, which have been rolled up, are laid over the sticks and opened out around the roof. Grassing starts at the bottom and continues upward. This first layer of grass is fastened through the thatching to the roof sticks, not as the grass on the granary roof was attached, which was fastened by ropes through the ledge. There is no ledge round a *d'aki* or any other hut. Only this first layer of grass is fastened to the roof sticks. When this is done, a second layer of grass overlaps the pinnacle of the roof and is tightly bound to it by eight or ten wrappings of hemp rope. For an average size hut, about twenty mats of grass are needed for the complete roofing. When it is finished the whole has a pleasantly symmetrical appearance.

The floor is the last thing to be done. About six inches of mud are packed on the ground and thoroughly saturated with water. This is then pounded with rocks to compact it and finally hand-smoothed to give a polished effect. Such a floor is left for three or four days before anyone may enter the hut.

Some *d'aki* (not guest huts or kitchens) have a raised floor, i. e. mud is packed in until the level of the floor is two or three feet above ground. In this case, the base of the doorway is also two or three feet above the ground, which means that one must step up to enter. The overall size of the hut is about the same, and as a result this kind of a hut has less room inside, but the advantage is that it is not susceptible to moisture and dampness during the rainy season, and the cold during the Harmattan season is also much ameliorated.

Occasionally there may be windows in a guest hut or a kitchen — very seldom in a *d'aki* — nobody wants people looking into their private living quarters! Windows are high up on the wall, and are thus protected by overhanging roofing grass from rain. They are made in the same way as doorways, i. e. either by blocking off a section with squared cornstalk, or by building the solid wall and then chopping out a section of the mud with an axe.

Doorways differ in height. Smaller ones may reach only four and a half feet, and two and a half to three feet wide.

The doorways of guest huts and kitchens are usually higher than those of *d'aki*, sometimes a bit more than five feet. Kitchens, like *d'aki*; only have one doorway. But guest huts always have two doorways, one opposite the other. Whenever it is too hot or there is no shade outside the compound, the guest hut is the accepted place for relaxation, and the two doorways catch even the slightest breeze.

Something that is becoming more frequent now — although still not common — are aluminum doors, which can be purchased in the market for ten shillings. There are simply a wooden frame to which an aluminum pan door has been hinged. The frame is inserted in the doorway and the sides are packed with mud. There is a latch on the door which can be locked to the frame.

Most Dukkawa 'close' their doors, however, by placing a thick grass mat outside the doorway. This mat is higher and wider than the doorway itself. Two sticks, about three feet high, are placed outside on the sides of the doorway about two or three inches away from the hut. Then the mat is slipped between the two sticks and the wall. Very often there is some sort of a wire hanging across the top of the doorway, overlapping it by about two feet on either side. The mat, which is already between the sticks and the doorway — on the bottom — is slid underneath the wire at the top, which holds it against the hut also. There are usually one or two wooden rings attached to this wire, and a piece of rope is strung through the grass mat, looped through the ring(s), and tied. This secures the mat firmly against the doorway. This is the way the 'door' is closed from the outside.

From inside, securing the mat against the doorway is a simpler matter. A piece of rope is strung through the center part of the mat, and is tied — on the inside of the hut — to a stick which is wider than the doorway. This stick is then twisted tighter and tighter, drawing the mat closer and closer until it is snug against the doorway, whereupon the stick is braced against the sides of the doorframe.

Doorways of *d'aki* and guest huts are usually decorated on the outside (Fig. 15). Sometimes these decorations are quite elaborate, spreading further away from the doorway along the walls. The designs are made by plastering mud onto the wall and then hand-moulding it to the desired pattern. Sometimes finger impressions are made in the plastering to add variety.

Fig. 15. Detail and decoration of a Dukku *daki*.

The mud plastering is about three quarters of an inch thick, varying in width from two to three inches.

When the plastering has dried, the entire area around the doorway is 'painted'. Pods from the locust bean tree are soaked in water, producing a deep reddish-brown liquid. This is then spread on the wall with bunches of dried grass, soaking into the mud and producing a smooth shiny surface. Sometimes just the area around the door is 'painted,' other times the entire outside of the hut is done this way.[8] This locust bean 'paint' is also used on the outside of a *rumbun mata* — the hut where women store their belongings — as well as on the inside wall of the guest hut.

Sometimes a man will make an overhead porch in front of the doorway of his *d'aki*. Two poles, about six feet in height, are placed on the sides of the doorway. Then two more poles, the same height, and the same distance apart from each other, are placed six or eight feet in front of the doorway. All of these poles are 'Y' forked at the top. First, two on one side of the doorway — the one next to the wall and the other six or eight feet away — are joined at the top by a branch placed in the fork, and tied in place. Then the same thing is done on to the two poles away from the hut.

When the tops of these four poles are thus joined rectangularly, long sticks are laid lengthwise upon them and roped to this frame. The extended roof serves a twofold purpose: first, it provides a shady area immediately outside the hut entrance, and the poles are strong enough so that items can be stored on top of it.[9]

Other Mud Construction.

In the *d'aki* — living quarters there is usually a mud bed, this being nothing more than a mud elevation of about ten inches from the floor, about six feet along one wall, and extending outward three or four feet.

---

[8] *Parkia Filicoidea*, the African Locust Bean Tree (Hausa: *Dorowa*). The liquid referred to above is called *makuba* and results from an actual fermentation that arises during the soaking process. Painting with *makuba* in the manner described, is an effective method of waterproofing mud buildings, and greatly prolongs their life and reduces maintenance, as well as giving a most pleasant appearance. *(Ed.)*

[9] This is a favorite place for storing bundles of *harawan wake* — bean fodder, much prized as a dry season feed for animals and therefore valuable either for use or sale. Bundles of corn are also sometimes temporarily stored in this manner after being taken out of the *rumbu* or if its capacity happens to be inadequate. Fig. 16 shows an example of this. *(Ed.)*

Fig. 16. An ornately decorated hut with a "patio" *(shirayi)* and guinea corn stored on its roof.

Sometimes, in a *d'aki*, there will also be a partition wall about four feet high, coming out from the sidewall as far as the center of the room. When entering the *d'aki*, the end of this wall is three or four feet inside the entrance. If there is such a wall, the mud bed — described in the paragraph above — is located behind it, hidden from the view of anyone who might happen to look into the hut.

Most guest huts (Hausa: *zaure*) just have a plain open floor. However, in some compounds the guest hut has a mud bed for the use of visitors who stay overnight. Also, in two or three guest huts which I have seen, there are mud chairs. These are simple mud constructions built up from the floor, against the wall, and are designed for one person to sit on.

In the kitchen hut there is always at least one grinding stone where the women grind the guinea corn into meal for cooking.

These are mud constructions — sometimes built on two or three stones at the base — which are about thirty inches high at one end, and two feet high at the lower end. This slant is purposely designed to assist the grinding  process. There is a mud lip at the lower end to prevent grain from falling off onto the floor. On the top surface of the mud, a flat stone is set in, and the grinding is done on this by means of a small stone which is held in both hands and rubbed up and down, crushing the grain between it and the grinding stone into a coarse flour. For details of this kind of mill, see Figs. 17 and 18.

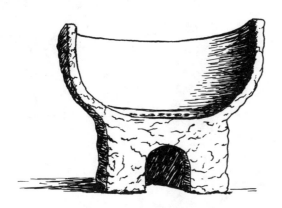

Fig. 17. Cross section of a typical Dukku hand-mill, showing details of construction.

Almost every compound has an oven for drying sheanuts and for smoking meat and fish. These are bowl-shaped mud constructions of which there are two types: open and closed, with an opening at the bottom where a fire can be made. The inside part of the bowl is perforated at the base with many small holes. The sheanuts or fish or meat are placed over these holes and the heat and smoke from underneath waft through them. See Figs. 19 and 20.

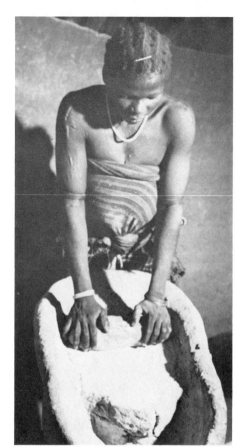

Fig. 18. Dukku woman grinding corn at a hand-mill.

Fig. 19. A closed hearth smoking and drying oven.

Fig. 20. An open hearth smoke oven. This is also used for cooking and for dry-ing shea nuts.

## C.  DOMESTIC UTENSILS

Every home, any place in the world, has common household objects which have practical value for everyday existence. The following items are found in every Dukku compound. These are not particularly used by the Dukkawa alone, but are common household utensils for all the tribes in the Yelwa area, and in many parts of Nigeria also.

*Mats.* Since it is not the custom of the people to sit on chairs, they sit — and sleep — on mats. There are two types of grass mats. The *tabarma* is made from thin palms — Phoenix Reclinata —[10]

---

[10] In actual fact, a wide variety of palm fronds are used for this purpose. In addi-tion to Phoenix R. (Hausa: *dabinon biri*), those commonly used are the Dum (or Ginger-bread) Palm, Hyphæne Thebaica *(goriba)* and the Deleb Palm, Borassus Flabellifer *(giginya),* also called the Fan Palm. This latter also provides heavily fibrous "timbers" which are termite proof amd much used in bigger buildings. *(Ed.)*

which are interwoven with each other. This pliable mat, which is usually about six feet by three feet, can be rolled up and will often be taken by a person when going on a trip so he will have something to sleep on regardless of where he has to spend the night. The other kind of grass mat *zana* is made from thicker, coarse grasses — Cymbopogon Ruprechtii and Andropogon.[11] It is usually square, or almost square, in shape and varies in size. A *zana* cannot be rolled up compactly — its stiffness, due to the coarse grass used in its manufacture preventing this — but its thickness makes it preferable for sleeping on during the Harmattan season when the ground, or the floor of the hut, is very cold. This *zana* mat is also the kind used for covering the *d'aki* doorway, as described previously.

Besides the grass mats, the skins of some animals are also treated to make mats. Those most commonly used are from cows, roan antelope, hartebeest, and rams.

A wooden *mortar* and *pestle* for pounding grain are essential. Another wooden item is the squat four-legged *stool* which women (not men) sit on when they are working. These are seldom more than 12 inches high and a large one would have a seat 12 inches by 18 inches. Most stools are smaller than this.

*Calabashes*[12] made from pear-shaped gourds are probably the most useful domestic utensils in a compound. The bottom part can be cut across to make calabash bowls, varying in size from four inches in diameter to more than two feet, and these "bowls" serve many needs. Food is always served in them; water for drinking and washing hands is brought in them; grain is winnowed by pouring it from one bowl (raised) into another on the ground; left-over food is stored in them; they are used to pour water over the body — a quick bath — when there is not time to go to the stream to wash; guinea corn beer is drunk from them; seeds for planting are carried in them; etc.

Sometimes just the top of a ten or twelve inch gourd is cut off to make a *water container* for traveling. A piece of rope is

---

[11] Most commonly Andropogon Guyanus (Hausa *gamba*). The Hausa for C. Ruprechtii is *k'yara*. (*Ed.*)

[12] Lagenaria Vulgaris (Hausa: *duma*), of which there are many shapes and varieties. (*Ed.*)

tied around the neck of the gourd and then extended long enough to be looped over the shoulder for easy carrying. When the gourd has been filled with water, the opening at the top is closed with a plug of leaves.

A smaller gourd, about four inches, is cut in the same manner and is used as a *tobacco container.* In this case, the top is cut very precisely so that it can be replaced to close the container (Fig. 21).

Other gourds are cut lengthwise to make spoons and ladles.

Fig. 21. Gourd water carrier and tobacco container.

Pottery.

Pots are made in different sizes and shapes for different purposes. Small open-faced ones — eight to ten inches in diameter — are used for cooking *miya*, the essential sauce or gravy made from meat, fish or vegetables and highly seasoned, into which the cooked grain is hand-dipped before being eaten. The *miya* will also be served in smaller clay bowls of this same type.

Larger open-faced clay pots — sometimes as tall as thirty inches — are used to cook the grain. The size of the pot depends upon the number of people for whom food is being cooked (Fig. 22).

Still larger open-faced clay pots are used for storing water in the compound. These can be three feet tall and hold about six gallons of water. Such a pot is usually set into the ground one-quarter or one-third of its length so that the water will remain as cool as possible. Frequently a water pot is located inside the kitchen hut or, if outside, is set in some shady spot and covered with a circular grass lid.[13]

Pots for carrying water[14] are spherical in shape with a small opening at the top (so the water will not spill when being transported). This type of pot is also used for storing beer or transporting it from one compound to another when there is a *biki*. They vary in size holding from two to four gallons of liquid.

Not all community living centers around the purely physical aspects of the home, and its creature comforts. The abstract considerations of the whole domestic economy also have to be taken into account.

The really essential, basic, needs of human existence can conveniently be grouped under four headings: —

1. Housing
2. Clothing
3. Food
4. Medicine.

---

[13] These discs of woven grass are known in Hausa as *faifai*. They vary in size from five or six inches to a couple of feet, and are used as calabash or pot covers, trays, platters for offering snacks, or even as fans. Such is the Hausa linguistic adaptability that the word also has a special modern meaning — phonograph record! *(Ed.)*

[14] Hausa *tulu*, pl. *tuluna*. *(Ed.)*

Fig. 22. A typical Dukku kitchen area. Beer cooking in the two large pots in the middle ground. A *tulu* (spherical pot for carrying water) stands on top of the water pot near the hut. A pot for cooking *tuwo* and two *miya* pots are at center foreground.

Fig. 23. Close up of the two beer pots, showing detail.

Housing and clothing, together with personal adornment, have already been dealt with. In a sense, they are as much a part of the communal reflection of a life-style as they are of the personal. Although it could be argued that this is also true of food, or of eating and drinking habits in general, such an argument is rejected here, since there is always a peculiarly "familial" intimacy in the preparation of food and the eating of it, which transcends (and in some cases negates) collective or societal mores. For this reason, food will be considered in detail in a later chapter.

There is, however, one aspect of the acquisition of the materials for the sustenance of life, which is peculiarly conditioned by societal or communal values. That is in the matter of the division of labor between the sexes. This question will therefore be considered next, after which, and in some respects as a natural corollary to it, the special place which hunting has in the Dukku life-style (both individual and collective) will also be examined.

Finally, to complete this section, brief consideration will be given to the Dukku concepts of curative medicine within the perceptions of the society as a whole, rather than within the personal perceptions of individual physical or spiritual well-being.

## CHAPTER FOUR

# DIVISION OF LABOR

## A.   MEN'S ACTIVITIES

Farming.

It can not be too highly stressed that the general pattern of the Dukku way of life is governed by the seasons. Generally it can be broken down in the following manner:

1. Farming: from the first rains in May until the harvesting is completed in November/December.

2. Compound repairs: repairing huts and fences, or building new ones.

3. Hunting: a month or two after the harvest, when everyone has had a chance to do the necessary work around their compounds, many men go off on hunting trips (four to six weeks).

4. Free time: most hunters return during the middle of the hot season and there is a lapse of about a month before the first rains permit them to start clearing their fields for the coming season.

| Month | J | F | M | A | M | J | J | A | S | O | N | D |
|---|---|---|---|---|---|---|---|---|---|---|---|---|
| Farming | | | | | x | x | x | x | x | x | x | x |
| Comp. repairs | x | x | | | | | | | | | | x |
| Hunting | | | x | x | x | | | | | | | |
| Free time | | x | x | x | x | | | | | | | |

There is necessarily some overlapping on the chart. Not every hunter goes on a long trip each year. Also, the necessary compound repairs vary from one compound to another.

The Dukkawa are primarily agriculturists. From the first rains in May until harvest time, every able-bodied man and boy farms. Women *never* work on the main farm. They may have a small patch of ground near the compound where they raise some guinea corn — for making beer — or some other crops, but this is more in the nature of 'gardening' than real farming. In this, Dukku women differ from women of some other tribes in the Yelwa area, such as the Gungawa and Kamberi, who sometimes work on the main farms as well as having small plots of their own.

For Dukkawa, the primary concern is the raising of guinea corn — *dawa*. The only objective they have during the farming season is to raise enough guinea corn to feed themselves through the next farming season. *Dawa* is the main ingredient in their staple food — *tuwo* — [1] which is eaten three times a day. . .every day of the year! *Tuwo* is simply guinea corn meal cooked with hot water — its texture is similar to that of grits, a coarse oatmeal. To eat it, *tuwo* is balled up in the hand, dipped into gravy — *miya* — and eaten. *Tuwo* can be made from guinea corn, millet, or rice, but the Dukkawa always prefer to use guinea corn, as long as it is available.

Once the primary importance of guinea corn is understood, consideration can then be given to the subsidiary crops which are grown. The following lists all the various crops which the Dukkawa grow, but it is certainly not meant to be implied that every BaDukku grows all of them. One which is commonly grown by most Dukkawa, however, is millet (Hausa: *gero*). They might not grow much of it, but the reason that they grow it at all is simple. Guinea corn takes four months to harvest; millet can be harvested in two and a half. If the last year's supply of guinea corn is running low, it can more quickly be supplemented by millet — from which *tuwo* can also be made — as against the extra month and a half which guinea corn takes to ripen. Millet is thus a stand-by crop.

---

[1] *Tuwo* is a very stiff porridge, so stiff that a piece scooped out of the communal dish with three fingers can quickly be formed into a ball about the size of a table-tennis ball. This is then dipped into the sauce *(miya)*, popped into the mouth and eaten. *(Ed.)*

Other crops are maize, groundnuts, sweet potatoes, beans, okra, beniseed, cassava, Bambarra groundnut (Hausa: *kwaruru*), and tobacco.[2]

Tobacco is highly valued among the Dukkawa. They are not unique in smoking, although, as a tribe, it appears that they smoke rather more than most others in the locality. They smoke both cigarettes and pipes. The cigarettes most commonly smoked are simply locally grown tobacco such as are made with newspaper — or any other kind of paper that is available. Twelve of these cigarettes can be purchased for a penny, whereas the cheapest manufactured cigarettes cost seven or eight pence for a package of twenty. Eighty-four local cigarettes can be bought for the same price as twenty manufactured ones (cheapest brand). Thus the reason for their popularity.

As *pipe-smokers,* the Dukkawa certainly have priority over any other tribe in the area. Dukkawa women do not smoke pipes or cigarettes, although some women chew tobacco. Some men and women also use snuff. It would seem, however, that at least half of the older men smoke pipes, although the tendency amoung younger men is to prefer cigarettes (Fig. 24).

Whatever use it is put to — pipe smoking, cigarettes, chewing, or snuff — the same kind of tobacco is used. There are two types locally grown: one plant produces a red flower, the other produces a white flower. The former kind is preferred.

Cash-crops are not viewed by the Dukkawa in terms of "Big Business", as is true of some other local tribes — most notably the onion farmers of the Gungawa. Among some Dukkawa, the attitude seems to be "If there is any left over, we can sell it." For

---

[2] Maize (Hausa *masara*), Zea Mays, of which half a dozen named varieties are known in Hausa: Groundnuts (peanuts), *gyad'a,* Arachis Hypogaea: Sweet Potato, *dankali,* Ipomoea Batatas, of which both the red and white varieties are known, the white being the commoner: Beans, *wake,* Vigna Sinensis, a dozen varieties having Hausa names: Okra, *kub'ewa,* Hibiscus Esculentus: Beniseed, *rid'i,* or *lid'i,* Sesamum Indicum, the common Sesame: Cassava (or Manioc), *rogo,* Manihot Palmata or M. Ultissima: Bambarra Groundnut, Voandezia Subterranea: Tobacco, *taba,* Nicotiana Tabacum, is widely grown, the leaves being chewed or smoked and the flowers, rubbed on the teeth whilst chewing certain varieties of kolanuts, stain them deep red, a much regarded procedure. *Gero,* Pennisetum Typhoideum, P. Spicatum, or P. Benthamii, has over a dozen named varieties in Hausa. (Ed.)

Fig. 24. Young man with pipe and bow.

others, certain crops are grown specifically to be sold, but not on a scale that is geared to make them rich. Sometimes guinea corn is sold when money is needed quickly, but this occasionally results in hardship before the next year's crop is ready. Those Dukkawa who grow groundnuts, maize, cassava, sweet potatoes, beans, and tobacco usually do so with a view to selling some, or much of them.

There is no special permission needed to farm a piece of land, except when someone wishes to work a plot which was formerly farmed by another. In that case he must contact the former occupier to obtain his approval. Other than this, there is no legal technicality which has to be followed. The Dukkawa are spread evenly throughout the bush, and obtaining farm land is not a problem.

The actual farming process consists of four stages. First, preparing the land; then planting; then weeding — which has periodically to be redone; and finally, the harvesting.

The clearing of the fields is started as soon as the first light rainfall occur, when the ground, which has been sun-baked to a cement-like hardness during the previous months, begins to show some signs of penetrability.

The planting is not done immediately. It is delayed until there are definite signs that the rainfall, even though light, will be frequent enough for the seeds to germinate. In one recent year there was an almost universal miscalculation. Three very heavy rainfalls occured at the end of May, which was taken to indicate an early rainy season, but then three weeks passed without another drop of water. All the planting had to be redone.

The most tedious task of the farming season is the weeding which is almost a continuous chore.

Then, depending on how early the crop was planted, and the kind of crop, the harvesting takes place anywhere from late October to December.

The Dukkawa use five kinds of farming tools. An axe, is used for clearing the fields. Large tree stumps are not removed. The Dukkawa just plant around them. Dukkawa have also been observed planting in areas where there are abandoned compounds. They do not bother to knock down the remnants of the former huts. They just plant up to the huts, around them, and continue on the other side!

Besides the axe, there are four different kinds of hoes, varying slightly in size and shape. The largest of these is the *garma*. The other three are *dunga, kalme,* and *fartanya*.[3] All of these hoes are short-handled, the handle being sixteen to eighteen inches long, which means that all farm work is done in a stoop position. (A common complaint at the beginning of every farming season is "I

---

[3] There are many synonyms for these names, depending largely on area. The basic patterns, however, remain much the same, if not identical, and undoubtedly represent a form of the ultimate in technological evolution *within the context of the culture.* (Ed.)

Fig. 25. A Dukku axe *(gatari)*.

Fig. 26. The plowing hoe *(garma)*.

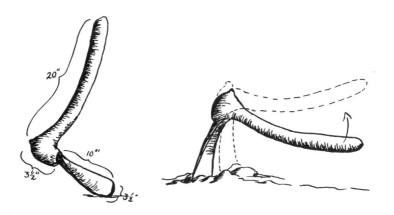

Fig. 27. The ridging hoe *(dunga)*.

Fig. 28. The *kalme* hoe.

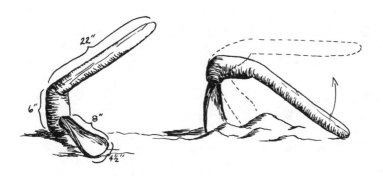

Fig. 29. A common tilling hoe *(fartanya).*

have a sore back.") These various implements are represented in figures 25—29.

The method of planting has been elevated almost to the status of an art. In one hand the farmer has a hoe, usually a *dunga;* in the other hand he holds a small calabash containing the seeds. In an almost simultaneous action, he strikes the ground with the hoe, flicks the seed(s) into the hole with the other hand, and covers it again with the hoe. It does not take more than two seconds! Guinea corn seeds are planted about two feet apart.

The Dukku farms are close to the compounds, sometimes adjacent to them, sometimes a little way away — but never more than a mile or two. Thus every night during the farming season the man will be at home. In this they differ from some other tribes — especially the Gungawa, and to some extent the Kamberi, whose farms are sometimes ten miles from their compounds. When it is time for clearing the fields, planting, etc., groups of their people will leave home for a week or ten days to stay in temporary huts near their farms. During the farming season it is common to go to a Gungawa compound, for instance, and be told that so-and-so had "gone to the farm," which means he might not be home for a week or so. With the Gungawa, there is a simple reason for this. In the Hausa language, *gungu* means *Island,* from which the Gungawa appropriated their name since they traditionally lived on the islands in the Niger River — which incidentally, are submerged now in the vicinity of Yelwa due to the recently built Kainji Dam which is located some sixty miles south of the town — as well as living along both banks of the River. Since the land along the river was not sufficient for all of them to farm, they had to move further away from the water to find good land which was not already being farmed by other people.

In a compound where there is more than one Dukku family — for example a father and two married sons — there will be one communal farm which the father and his sons will work together. Besides this, each son will have his own smaller farm to supply extra food or for growing cash-crops.

A common practice among all farmers in this area — not just Dukkawa — is "burning the bush." In late December or January, when everyone has finished harvesting their crops, the remaining cornstalks will be burnt. This is always done at night when there is the least wind, to minimize the chances of the fire getting out of control near the grass roofs of the compound huts. It is believed that the cornstalk ashes act as fertilizer for the ground.

Once a year there is an Agriculture Show in Yelwa town to which all the people in the Yauri Emirate are invited. All kinds of crops, animals, handcrafts, etc. are brought to this exhibition and, after a general viewing, judges award prizes for the best in each category. After the awards have been distributed, several talks are given to the people by various officials, one of whom is usually an Agricultural Officer. In the four years that this Agricultural Show was attended it was always explained to the people that they should *not* burn the cornstalks after the harvest. It is true that by doing this a few minerals are returned into the soil, but it would be much more effective if the stalks were left gradually to rot. Also, cornstalks harbor various kinds of insects which provide added nutrients to the soil. But old customs die slowly, and there is still a lot of "burning the bush." Chemical fertilizer[4] can be pruchased in the market — eight to ten shillings for a fifty-six pound bag — but the Dukkawa do not use it. Besides burning the cornstalks, the only other method they use to replenish fertility is to tether their cattle — for those who have them — on the farm area during the Dry Season.

Fallowing is not practiced other than in a rather haphazard manner. After farming a piece of land for two or three years, a Ba-Dukku will merely extend his farm by clearing land adjacent to it. The next year he might extend it a bit more. After that he either continues to extend his farm — if the land can be easily cleared — or returns to the first section which was temporarily abandoned.

The custom of *gayya* — communal labor — is an interesting one.[5] If a farmer finds that he does not have enough time to clear

---

[4] Known as *takin Turawa* (manure from Europe) and specially formed into pellets to deliver a fixed dose to each planting point as described above, artificial fertilizer was introduced about 1950. The results in the heavily populated areas of Sokoto Province especially were spectacular, largely due to the efforts of one Administrative Officer whose advocacy of the program was enthusiastic. It was never expected to appeal to groups like the Dukkawa, where there is no shortage of land available, but there is demand for it in Yelwa itself. *(Ed.)*

[5] The word *gayya* in itself is also extremely interesting, packed with socio-political

all the land that he wants to plant, or if the harvesting is too much for him to do alone, he will invite his neighbors and friends to come and help him for one day. This is also a semi-social event. No wages will be paid, but guinea-corn beer will be provided for everyone who comes to work. Sometimes a drummer is called (he gets paid) to supply 'background music' of a suitable tempo. At the end of the day, everyone goes home happy. The workers have had their beer and a social get-together, and the farmer has got his work done.

As mentioned above, there is a lapse of some time between clearing the farm land, as soon as the land is workable, and the planting of the seeds, when the rains have become sufficiently frequent so that there is no danger the seeds will die. There is also another lapse of time after the planting is done and the grass is high enough to need weeding. During these two intervening times, many Dukkawa will often go in search of work on others' farms to earn some extra money. If they are fortunate to find a job for a couple of weeks they could make up to two pounds (about five dollars) which would be a substantial added-income for them.

## Domestic Animals

Some domestic animals are kept for utility, others are raised for food or to be sold.

Every compound has several dogs. Some of the larger compounds have as many as ten. The main purpose of having dogs is for protection against thieves. At night, they announce the arrival of visitors as they approach the compound, since it is almost impossible to enter a compound and escape their notice. Another very practical use for dogs is hunting. They are especially effective in chasing monkeys and forcing them to 'tree' until the hunter can arrive. The Dukkawa eat monkeys. Some Dukkawa men (but not women) eat dogs.

---

implications. Originally, it meant "the fyrd" in the true Saxon sense of the *levée en masse* for military purposes. Gradually it came to mean any form of communal labour or activity, and, in the latter days of the Colonial Power, as a result of the international sensitivity to any connotations of "forced" labour, the whole concept of *gayya* was greatly frowned on. There is no evidence, however, that the populace as a whole ever rejected its basic premises, as the example quoted very clearly shows. (Ed.)

Cats are not numerous — probably because it is difficult completely to domesticate them and keep them in the compound — but a BaDukku will never pass up the opportunity to get a kitten and try to train it. It is a proven fact that cats are one of the best safeguards against snakes, which constitute one of the greatest fears of the people living in bush. As mentioned in the section on clothing, skins of large cats are used to make loincloths for young boys.

Another useful animal is the donkey. This beast-of-burden is used whenever there are too many loads — or the loads are too heavy — to be transported by the people themselves. They are expensive by Dukkawa standards, costing about ten pounds, so not every compound has one. But larger compounds, where several families live together, will usually have at least one.

Only rarely will a BaDukku own a horse. Possibly they were more common in former times as a means of transportation for long distances, but today they have little more than prestige value. Because of the tsetse fly, horses are difficult to keep healthy in this area and are of little or no importance as work animals; and, no matter how far away his destination may be, a BaDukku will almost always walk (a few Dukkawa have second-hand bicycles).[6]

Most Dukkawa possess goats and/or sheep. These are raised for commercial purposes. The people themselves almost never slaughter one of the goats or sheep for their own use.

The most common fowl are chickens, guinea fowl, and (in a few compounds) pigeons. These are mainly raised to be sold, although the people do eat them on occasion.

A BaDukku's economic status is determined by cattle, but not in the sense of how many cows are owned. The Dukkawa are not herdsmen (in one large compound which is considered — by the Dukkawa themselves — as the "richest" compound in the vicinity, eight brothers own fifteen head of cattle, no one person having more than two for himself). The simple fact that a Dukku man owns a cow, whose value is about twenty pounds (fifty-plus dol-

---

[6] Historically, it would have been quite unusual for the Dukkawa to have owned horses. Quite apart from the trypanosomiasis threat (which was very real), the use of the horse in war, which constituted the *real* reason for their maintenance in pre-colonial times, did not accord with the Dukku defensive strategies. *(Ed.)*

lars), immediately classifies him financially as being in the upper bracket. Ordinarily it is only large compounds, where several families live together, where the people own cows. Usually a father and his adult sons will jointly invest in purchasing a couple. Single-family compounds, or young married men, are considered prosperous if they own a few goats or sheep.

Crafts.

The concept of a craftsman as a professional tradesman who makes his livelihood from practicing his trade and not doing anything else, has no application to the Dukkawa. During the rainy season, *every able-bodied Dukku man farms.* The various crafts are considered purely as secondary occupations to be pursued when there is no farming. Among the Dukkawa, there are three groups of craftsmen, their trades being more practical than artistic in nature.

1. *Blacksmiths.* Keen hunters as they are, it is natural that some Dukkawa would be blacksmiths. Metal is needed to fix gun barrels in stocks, make trigger mechanisms, fashion arrowheads, and to make knives and matchets, all of which have a very practical value. Blacksmiths, besides this, also make many kinds of simple jewelry such as earrings, nose-tacks, finger rings, bracelets, etc.[7]

2. *Leather-workers.* Leather working, like smithing, is a practical trade which fulfills a definite need within the culture. The most common items made are bags, loincloths, knife sheaths, sword and matchet sheaths, bowstrings, men's belts, and neck cords for holding charms, which are also contained in leather packets.

3. *Wood-work.* This craft has limited application, being confined mainly to the making of mortars and pestles and the small wooden stools for women previously described, handles for hoes and axes, and for making pipes.

Pipes are made from the wood of the *kiriya* tree — Prosopis oblonga — or the *taura* tree — Detarium sengalense. An adze is used to shape the outside of the pipe; then a small metal arrow is worked through the center of the stem of the pipe for the inhaling

---

[7] As well as all agricultural implements, of course. *(Ed.)*

of smoke; and, finally, the bowl of the pipe is carved out with a knife. Sometimes no bit is attached to the end of the stem, but usually there is some sort of metal tip. All of the following have been seen being used for bits; bicycle tire valves, short sections of umbrella shafts, bicycle pedal shafts, and discarded rifle cartridges. Certain kinds of bone are also used, and probably were much more widely used in former days.

Every Dukku pipe smoker has his own "lighter" which is the basic flint-and-steel. A piece of tinder is placed on a small stone, and this is struck with a metal hammer. When the tinder sparks it is put on the tobacco and pressed down.

Dukkawa clean their pipe stems with a thick piece of straw. Those who are fortunate enough to obtain one, use a bicycle tire spoke for this purpose.

## B.   WOMEN'S ACTIVITIES

Most of the work which women do pertains to the domestic — i. e. caring for the family and household — rather than the economic, and as such will be dealt with more fully in the chapter on Domestic Life. At present, therefore, only those aspects which have an economic value in as much as they are a source of income, or which supply needs which would otherwise have to be satisfied from elsewhere, will be considered.

### Pottery

Pots for cooking *miya,* for cooking *tuwo,* for carrying water, and for storing water are made by some Dukku women. They also make calabashes of all sizes and shapes.

### Cookery

There are several kinds of food which Dukku women make, and then take to market to sell.

1.  *k'osai*: these are small cakes made from bean flour.
2.  *dak'uwa*; this is made from guinea-corn flour and ground-nuts.
3.  *k'ulik'uli*: donut-shaped cakes made from peanuts.

One item which all Dukkawa make is shea butter. This is a seasonal occupation during the months of May to August. Almost every day during this period the women and girls will go through the bush gathering sheanuts. They are brought home and dried — in the mud 'ovens' described in Chapter Three — and then pounded. After pounding, they are cooked into an oil.[8] Sheanut oil has multiple uses, the main one being as a cooking oil. It can also be used for treating leather — as mentioned when describing how loincloths are made — as well as for making soap and pomade, and as a fuel into which a wick is placed to serve as a source of light.

Making *guinea-corn beer,* however, is probably the Dukku women's most substantial source of income. It can always be sold on market-days (there are usually two or three markets a week at various places within reach of a Dukku compound), and it is always in great demand at *biki.*

There is a special process for making this beer. First, the guinea-corn is put in cold water and left for one day. The following day the guinea-corn is removed and washed — by putting it in a basket and pouring water through. This is done to remove any bad odor. Then the corn is spread on the floor of a hut and covered with sheanut leaves so that it can germinate. It is left thus for two or three days, after which it is taken outside and spread in a sunny place to dry. Ordinarily it is spread on the ground; during the rainy season it is placed on a mat.

After it has dried, the corn is rubbed to remove the husks and then it is winnowed. After winnowing, the corn is ground into meal, which is poured into cold water and stirred. It is allowed to set this way for about an hour, during which time the thicker sediment settles to the bottom. Now the top third — the thinner part — is removed and the remaining, thicker, two-thirds is cooked for two hours, being continually stirred, lest it burn due to its consistency. After cooking in this way, the uncooked thin portion, which had been removed, is mixed back into the cooked portion and left to set until the following day.

The next day, the top third is again separated. This thin portion is further divided in half. One half is then cooked for about

---

[8] Shea-butter, indeed, has always been in steady demand on the fats and edible oil commodity exchanges. It makes excellent pastries. *(Ed.)*

an hour until, due to evaporation, only a very small amount remains. A quantity of cornstalk ash is then mixed into this to make it very thick. This is called *namijin giya* (an interesting name, since *namiji* means "male" and *giya* means "beer" thus, "the male of the beer!")[9]

While the *namijin giya* is being made, the other two-thirds is filtered through a basket — since it is still too thick to be drunk — and pressed in the hands. Then the half of the thin portion which was *not* cooked — i. e. not the *namijin giya* — is poured back into this larger quantity, and the whole is then cooked for three hours, after which the *namijin giya* is also added to it. After being well stirred together, it is allowed to set for one day, and as it sets, it begins to bubble, which denotes that fermentation is taking place.

The next day the liquid is again filtered through a basket to remove any excess bran. Some people may be allowed to taste it after this. Its alcoholic content is still low and the drink is very sweet. Even small children like it. This "near beer" is then put in clay pots to set for another day — continuing to ferment — until it becomes proper beer. The entire process thus takes about ten days.

When the beer is attested to be ready, everyone on the compound will get a free taste. After that, the rest is sold. If the woman herself bought the guinea-corn, she will keep all the money she makes from the sale of the beer. If her husband purchased the corn, or gave it to her from the corn he had harvested, he will receive the money, but has to give his wife some money for her work.

With very few exceptions, all Dukku men and women drink this guinea-corn beer. Young boys and girls drink it, and small babies are even given a taste. One shilling (13 to 15 cents) buys about two quarts of guinea-corn beer. It is something of an acquired taste!

---

[9] *Namiji* is a complicated word. In addition to meaning "male", it also means "one who strengthens" or "the impregnator of" or, even, *fons et origia*. In this case the phrase *namijin giya* clearly means "that which *starts* [i. e. impregnates] the beer by beginning the process of fermentation. *(Ed.)*

## CHAPTER FIVE

# HUNTING

## HUNTING IN GENERAL

According to tribal tradition, all Dukku men consider themselves born and bred to hunt. More importantly, neighboring tribes (Kamberi, Gungawa, Shangawa, Sarkawa, Hausa) all acknowledge their expertise and respect the Dukkawa as being the best hunters in the area. Their reputation extends far beyond the confines of their domicile. As far south as Jebba (200+ miles) and to the Dahomey border in the west people can be found who have heard of Dukku hunters.

From their reputation, one might with justice conclude that they are full-time hunters and nothing else. This is not true. In fact, as has been shown they are full-time farmers. But the farming season in the Yelwa area, for the crops which the Dukkawa grow, (guinea corn, millet, maize) is only seven months long and it is during the five non-farming months from January to May that the hunting is done. When the harvesting of guinea corn is finished in December the most pressing concern is the repairing of huts, or the building of new ones, before the next rainy season. Because of the Harmattan, the months of December through February are the coolest months of the year so the repairing of compounds is usually begun as soon as the harvest has been completed. Depending upon the repairs and rebuilding required to be done, the work can take anything from a couple of weeks to two months. But there will always be some time remaining before the next farming season for those who want to go hunting.

Because of the general lack of large game animals in the areas where they live, the Dukkawa travel as far as one hundred and fifty miles on their hunting trips. The most common hunting grounds

66

are west of the Niger River in the Borgu Division of Kwara State, although every year a few Dukkawa head southward beyond Kontagora. Not all Dukku men go on hunting trips every year, but it would be exceptional to find an adult BaDukku who has not made several trips.

There are some signs, that this might change in the not too distant future. As the good hunting areas become further away, and as more outside influences bear upon traditional customs, the heritage of hunting in the Dukku culture may lose something of its present stature.[1]

In the areas where the Dukkawa hunt, there are found the following animals: elephant, dwarf buffalo, roan antelope, hartebeest, waterbuck, warthog, kob, bushbuck, reedbuck, red-fronted gazelle, oribi, crested duiker, and red duiker. The Dukkawa have their own classification of "Big" and "Small" animals. "Big Animals" include elephant, dwarf buffalo, roan antelope, hartebeest, and waterbuck . . . . in that order. Some Dukkawa do not consider the waterbuck a "Big Animal," even though a male waterbuck might weigh over five hundred pounds. The criteria for the classification "Big Animal" among those of approximately the same size depend on the beast's sagacity and the difficulty in killing them — endurance, speed, fortitude etc.

Since hunting is a tradition common to all Dukku men, there is no classification of hunters and non-hunters. But the above categorization of "Big Animals" and "Small Animals" does serve to distinguish the better hunters from the mediocre. A man who kills two "Big Animals" will have somewhat more respect than a hunter who kills only one. A hunter who kills a roan antelope will be mentioned before the hunter who kills a waterbuck.

If a hunter kills an elephant, a special *biki* will be prepared

---

[1] It is still possible to note, however, how tribes with an even stronger hunting tradition than the Dukkawa, in that their annual *farauta* (hunt) is communal (e. g. the Bachama of Numan Division) still cling to the custom despite the virtual absence of any game at all! It may be, therefore, that there is more in such practices than is immediately apparent. Indeed, the element of "ritual fulfillment" in customs of this nature is becoming increasingly recognised. F. Barth in respect of the Ru'alla and E. Peters in respect of the Bedouins of Cyrenaica have drawn attention to similar phenomena. In such cases, it appears that "the medium is the message" *(Ed.)*

for him. [2] Among the other Big Animals, if a hunter kills three within one year, a *biki* must be made for him also. If a hunter kills two Big Animals, a *biki* may or may not be prepared for him (although if one of the two animals is a buffalo, it is almost certain that there would be a *biki*).

It is interesting to note that though there is a greater public celebration when an elephant is killed, yet among the Dukku hunters themselves the killer of a buffalo is considered the better hunter. The buffalo is considered the most dangerous animal that is hunted; therefore special recognition is accorded.[3]

The lion is called the "friend of the hunter" and, as such, is not hunted by the Dukkawa. When it was suggested to one hunter the term "friend of the hunter" merely served as an excuse to avoid confrontation and that they were really afraid to hunt lions, his answer was simple and very realistic. "We hunt buffalo. Who can say we are afraid of lions? "

*Sarkin Daji* — King of the Bush — is the title bestowed by the Dukkawa on the man considered to be the best hunter in the entire area. It is strictly an honorary recognition with no other benefits, although to be considered the best hunter among the best tribe of hunters is no small honor in itself!

Because the Dukku hunters travel long distances for their hunting trips, they do not hunt with dogs since there would be the problem of feeding them. Nor do they use traps to capture animals since they are constantly moving from one area to another and lack any opportunity to return to check the traps.

Nowadays all of the hunters have guns although the older men recall the days when they did all of their hunting with bow and arrow. Some hunters will still take a bow as a precautionary measure in the event of their guns being damaged.

The desire for hunting never dies for a Dukku man. As long as he is capable of walking the necessary distance he is likely to go on a hunting trip. Even if his eyes are poor and he cannot see well,

---

[2] I know of six different men who have killed at least one elephant.

[3] A view, indeed, which is shared by *all* big game hunters, who regard the African Buffalo in all its sub-species (in this case the Congo Dwarf Buffalo, Bos Caffer Nanus or Syncerus Caffer Planiceros (*b'auna*)) as the most cunning, mean, and dangerous animal in the bush. (*Ed.*)

an older hunter who can still travel the distance might attach himself to a hunting group, not to do any actual hunting but to be on hand to butcher the animal and smoke the meat while the younger hunters continue the hunt. Boys as young as ten years of age are also sometimes taken to be taught the techniques of tracking and stalking animals. One of the six Dukkawa hunters refered to above as being known to have killed an elephant is a fifteen year old boy.

There are various charms which Dukku hunters may or may not use. Very little, if any, significance is attached to these. For some it is part of the symbolism of hunting, for others it is a continuation of tradition dating from days when their fathers and grandfathers placed a more superstitious value on various hunting charms.[4]

But there is one charm whose efficacy is acknowledged by all Dukku hunters (as well as every hunter encountered from various other tribes throughout Nigeria, Niger, and Dahomey.) This is *baduhu,*[5] which literally means "to make dark". It is mainly used when hunting elephant and buffalo, and is accorded the power of making the hunter invisible − or, at least, difficult to be seen − so that he can get close enough to get a good shot. Thus, it has a two-fold advantage, namely one of giving the hunter luck in killing dangerous animals and the other of protecting him from serious harm or even death. As far as could be ascertained, no Dukku hunter will attempt to hunt an elephant without *baduhu.* Although it is preferable to have *baduhu* for buffalo, a few hunters have killed this animal without it.

One of the better Dukku hunters who has killed eight Big Animals − roan antelope and hartebeest − in the last three years, wants to kill an elephant but will not go after one until he gets *baduhu.* He is a confident hunter and concedes that he could probably safely kill an elephant even without having the charm. What he

---

[4] This attitude would seem to bear out the view expressed in fn. 1 above. *(Ed.)*

[5] The belief in *Ba duhu* is ubiquitous, not only among hunters but the general public. The Thief Guilds, the existence of which, though hotly denied, cannot be doubted, are especially credited with having most efficacious receipes. One prime ingredient is a substance which is found in large termite hills. An alternative translation of *baduhu* would be "invisible man", and this interpretation seems to be supported by the fact that possessors of the charm are often collectively termed *'Yan duhu. (Ed.)*

fears is that some misfortune would then befall his family or his compound. So it seems the effect of *baduhu* is more far-reaching than being merely a lucky charm for the hunter himself.

The *baduhu* charm consists of a cloth packet about three inches in diameter. It can either be square or triangular in shape. Into this packet are sewn small sealed pockets, as many as ten, each containing a different ingredient — really a separate charm. Some might consist of the powdered bark of various kinds of trees, a small piece of dried skin of some animal, or a few hairs of others. It is difficult to tell exactly what the charm contains because usually the hunters themselves do not know. They obtain it from only the most reputable of hunters, usually the *Sarkin Daji,* and he may not tell the recipient anything more than that it is a good charm whilst at the same time giving him advice on how to hunt the more dangerous animals. A *baduhu* charm is made individually for each particular hunter, so even if the hunter is given any explanation of the ingredients, it becomes a very personal thing and he is unlikely to tell anyone else.

Not every hunter who requests *baduhu* gets it. Since the reputation of the person who makes the charm depends upon its effectiveness, the charm-maker will usually only agree to provide it for those hunters of proven ability and desire who will probably get the animals they go after.

WEAPONS

**Guns**

The guns used by the Dukku hunters are long-barreled muskets which are locally made. The barrel is made from a piece of one-half to one inch galvanized water pipe. Although not readily available, the most desired barrel of all, however, is made from an old vehicle drive-shaft which has been especially drilled for this purpose. The metal pipes which are used for making gun barrels can usually be purchased in the market. Their length is generally between three and four feet. The stock of the gun is made by a wood carver to any specification the hunter desires. The barrel is then attached to this stock either by metal bands or by strips

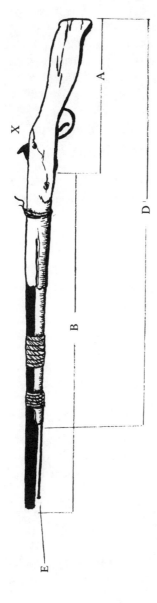

KEY

Darkly shaded parts are made of iron.
Lightly shaded parts are leather bands.
Unshaded parts are the wooden portions.

Fig. 30. A typical Dukku hunter's gun, showing details of construction.

Total Length = c. 4' 10"

A = 1 ft. 4" (A is butt end of the gun.)
B = 3 ft. 5" (B is iron.)
C = 10"
D = 3 ft. 10" (D is wood.)
E = 9½" protruding (E is iron rod.)

At its widest point, the wooden material measures about 3" and 1" at its narrowest point.
The iron tubing has its widest end buried in the wooden material (at X) which is about 2" wide.
At its narrowest the tubing is 5/6 of an inch approximately.

of rawhide which are stitched together. After this treated leather dries it provides a very firm grip. The trigger mechanism is hand-forged and hinged onto the stock. The firing apparatus is fashion-ed as a leaf-spring; a strong piece of metal being bowed out to give the spring effect. All of the metal work is made by blacksmith. The pipe used for the barrel costs twenty to thirty shillings ($3.00—$4.50). If a new gun is bought completely made, it costs sixty to eighty shillings ($9.00—$12.00). See figure 30 for details of the construction of such a gun.

Gunpowder charcoal is made from tree bark. The bark is burned and then pounded, after which it is mixed with sulphur and saltpetre.

When hunting, the guns are loaded by pouring a certain a-mount of powder into the barrel of the gun, and then compressing it with a small piece of soft cloth or cotton. Bits of metal or shot are then added, and finally another wad in the form of a piece of cloth or cotton to keep everything in place.

The tips of two or three ordinary wooden matches are then broken off and placed into the insert of the firing mechanism. The piece of metal used as a firing-pin will not be inserted, however, until an animal is seen and the hunter gets ready to shoot. Insert-ing the firing-pin and releasing the trigger mechanism ignites the spark and discharges the gunpowder.

When aiming his gun at an animal, the Dukku hunter does not cradle the stock against his shoulder nor rest his cheek along-side it to sight down the barrel. The guns are not by any means precision weapons and they can easily backfire (usually from an overload of gunpowder) so the hunter strives to keep his face as far as possible from the firing mechanism. The hand holding the base of the stock will extend as far as it can from his body, and the forefinger of the other hand will grasp the trigger. With the gun extended in front of him, a hunter will sight the animal along the barrel and then turn his head to the side an instant before he releases the trigger (Fig. 31).

* * *

Fig. 31. A Dukku hunter on the point of firing his locally made gun.

## Bows and Arrows.

Every Dukku boy has a bow and at least one arrow. He knows that it is not simply a toy because from his earliest recollections he can remember the hunters going off on hunting trips with their guns and bows, and later returning with meat killed by those same weapons. He sees other boys a little older than himself who can all shoot arrows with reasonable accuracy, going off from the compound and sometimes returning with a hare or bush rat or even a small bird. He sees, rather than is told, that hunting is part of the Dukku way of life. So one of the first things a Dukku boy learns to do, and to do well, is to use a bow and arrow.

Fig. 32. Detail of the bowman's grip.

Fig. 33. Dukku hunter with his hunting bow. The long arrow in the quiver, of which there is always one, is *never* poisoned. It is intended for non-lethal self protection and is made long so that it can be immediately distinguished, by touch if necessary. *(Ed.)*

The bows themselves are very simple. The stave, which is stiff and bends very little, is about five feet long for a proper hunting bow. A boy's bow will be somewhat shorter. A leather bowstring is tied to one end of the bow and then drawn tightly through a notch at the other end, wrapped around several times, and tied. Because of the straightness of the wood that is used, the bowstring is a maximum of three inches from the bow at its center point. Some Dukkawa make their own bows, but because the more preferable kinds of wood are not to be found in the immediate area, completely made bows are sometimes purchased in the market. Most often the wooden stave is bought in the market and the BaDukku completes the rest of the work himself. A completed bow costs three to five shillings (40¢ − 60¢) (Figs. 32 and 33).

Arrowheads are forged by blacksmiths from six-inch pieces of metal. There are various patterns of barbs. The three most common are the single-barb, the double-barb, and one with several small barbs on both sides (Figure 34). The six-inch shank is one-eighth inch in diameter tapering to a point opposite the barbed end. This pointed end can either be inserted into a fifteen inch shaft (usually of bamboo) or fastened alongside it. In either case it is secured in place by thin leather strips which have been treated with sheanut oil to improve elasticity.

Poison is always used on arrows when the Dukkawa are hunting. There are three different kinds of plants whose roots are used to make the poison. Any of these roots can be pounded and then mixed with the seeds of a certain type of small wild melon. This is cooked in a small amount of water until the entire mixture becomes very thick and turns black. The tips of the arrows are then dipped into this mixture and left to dry. Even after two or three months this dried poison does not lose its effectiveness.[6]

For shooting elephants, a much longer arrow is shot from a gun. This is the only way an elephant can be killed. An arrow shot from a bow would not have sufficient force to penetrate the elephant's thick skin so that the poison could take effect and ordinary metal pellets shot from a gun would not strike with suffi-

---

[6] For some discussion of arrow poison, see Muffett, "The Sokoto Caliphate" in Crowder *West African Resistance;* Hutchinson, London, & Africana, New York, 1971. *(Ed.)*

Fig. 34. Three common Dukku arrowheads.

cient force to reach a vital part of the elephant's body. A piece of cloth is tied tightly around the shaft of the arrow with leather strips, and six to eight inches of this are then dipped in the poison until the cloth is saturated. The force of the gun will project the sharp arrowtip beyond the thick layer of skin and the barb prevents the poisoned tip from falling out. The most desired point of entry is the relatively soft skin between the elephants hind legs.

HUNTING TRIPS.

The first thing a Dukku hunter does when he decides he will go on a hunting trip is to attach himself to one of the groups that he knows will be going. Some hunters go every year so he will naturally inquire among them. A large hunting party can consist anything from ten to twenty men. Sometimes, however, three or four neighboring Dukkawa will decide to go off by themselves and not join a larger group. These plans will be made long in advance of the time of departure since they anticipate the trip in much the same way as a family in America plans a vacation. They settle which area to go to and approximately how long they will spend away from home. Larger groups tend to hunt for a longer period of time, some up to six weeks. If they are successful, some of the hunters will return early with the meat while the others continue to hunt.

One crucial decision concerns the exact date of departure. It is calculated according to what time of the month when there will be the least moonlight at night. The reason for this is that most Dukkawa hunt after dark with a carbide head-light as well as hunting during the daytime. The head-light is most effective when there is no moonlight at all. The beam of light will penetrate further into the darkness and the eyes of animals can be seen at greater distances. Also, there is less chance that the shadowed form of the hunter will be seen by the animal. Most game animals are fascinated by the glare of light and will continue to look at it as long as they can see nothing else. The only real exception to this is the warthog which instinctively turns away from light. If an animal detects the presence of a hunter, however, it will run.[7]

The carbide head-lights which the Dukku hunters use are imported and cost approximately eighty shillings ($12.00). Each consists of a double container, the bottom part containing calcium carbide (which can be purchased in the market) and the top part containing water. A knob at the top regulates the amount of water which drips onto the carbide and produces acetylene gas. A shiny concave copper disc about ten inches in diameter is fastened onto the front of the double container and this whole apparatus is then attached to a cap which is made especially for this purpose. When the water regulator is opened and the gas begins to emerge, it is ignited with a match and the light is then reflected and projected by the copper disc.

Basic hunting equipment consists of a gun, gunpowder, bullets, small pieces of cloth or cotton, a knife, a two-foot matchet, and a large bag to carry accessories such as tobacco, matches, kola nuts, etc. Some hunters will also take a bow and some arrows.

The only food that is taken on the trip is cassava flour and sugar. When this is mixed with water it makes a substantial gruel.

---

[7] This method of hunting is, of course, completely illegal and is forbidden under the Game Laws. *(Ed.)*

Later yams can be purchased at small villages near the hunting area. Then, hopefully, there should be meat!

When the hunters leave on a hunting trip they will follow the same general routes to the various areas. March is the month that most of the hunters leave, and this is the beginning of the Hot Season. It has also been more than four months since the last rainfall, so the general routes they follow pass through places where they will find water.

When they reach the hunting area, the hunters will camp together, but hunt separately. They know the area well enough so that they can designate definite places where they will meet at the end of the day. If it is a large hunting group, when they arrive at the hunting area, they will probably separate into two or three smaller groups and move off in different directions. Calculating by the moon, they may decide to meet after a certain number of days at a particular place, or each group might decide to go its own way and not rendevous with the others again.

When shooting the larger animals — buffalo, roan antelope, hartebeest or waterbuck — a Dukku hunter will get as close as possible to his quarry, and always try to aim at one of the front legs. If it happens that the bullets do not reach the heart or lungs, a broken front leg will hamper the animal's movements sufficiently for the hunter to reload his gun for a second shot, which this time will be aimed at the neck. An animal with a broken hind leg can run almost as fast as if not wounded, and can travel several miles before having to stop for rest.

There is no prayer or special ritual to be observed when cutting an animal's throat. But there is a particular dance for each of the "Big Animals" and this will be performed before the butchering of the animal begins. Although the hunters hunt separately, several are usually in the same vicinity, and a loud shout brings them together. While they all do the dance, which takes about five minutes, the other hunters sing the praise of the one who killed the animal. These songs are not prescribed songs, but rather, represent each hunter's own version of the killing of the animal, and of the successful hunter's prowess.

After the animal is skinned and butchered, the meat is cut into thin strips, and hung up to dry in a shady place. Meanwhile, trees and branches are cut to make a platform (about two feet high) on which the meat will be smoked. Preparing it in this way over a small fire takes six to eight hours.

When the hunt is over and the hunters decide to head for home, some of the meat will be wrapped in the skins. The remainder will be divided and tied with a bark which is stripped from reeds and knotted together to serve as a rope.

## CHAPTER SIX

# MEDICINE

## A.  DISEASES

First, it is as well to have some understanding of the particular diseases which beset the area in which the Dukkawa live. Besides the ordinary sicknesses and ailments which are common to people everywhere — e. g. headache, upset stomach etc. — there are special hazards which afflict people living in this part of Nigeria, and specifically in the area under consideration.

Parasitic Diseases

> *Malaria* — malignant tertian and quartan malaria — is prevalent. During the past five years, several doctors and laboratory technicians have spent periods of time in Yelwa doing various investigations on different aspects of this disease, and a general consensus of their opinions is that roughly 50 percent of the children in the bush areas die from this disease before they attain the age of three. Those who survive past this age gradually develop a natural immunity to malaria — in as much as this is possible.
> *Amoebiasis.* This is a very common cause of dysentery, which is distinct from the type of diarrhoea which also occurs frequently.
> *Bilharziasis* — Schistosoma Haemotobium and Schistosoma Mansoni — is a frequent cause of infection.
> *Onchocerciasis,* a form of filariasis, is a very common disease causing itching and joint pains. It is also known as "River Blindness", and much of the local blindness, the incidence of which is high, may be ascribed to this cause.

Owing to the nature of the diseases, both bilharziasis and onchocerciasis are more prevalent in areas near water. Both are much more common in the immediate area of Yelwa — which is situated on the eastern bank of the Niger River — than they are in the sectors where the Dukkawa live, which are further inland (four or five miles from the river at the nearest point).

Infectious Diseases

*Lobar pneumonia* is common, especially coming into evidence in the late Harmattan season and early hot season.
*Cerebro-spinal Menengitis* and *Measles* are both epidemic diseases.
*Smallpox* was an epidemic disease until recently, but a successful medical campaign appears now to have virtually eradicated it as such.
*Tuberculosis* is quite a common disease, both pulmonary and other forms.

Poisonous Snakes

Bites by the *Carpet Viper* — Echis Carinatus — and the *Night Adder* — Causus Phombeatus — are especially common in the areas where Dukkawa live!
The *Black-hooded Spitting Cobra* is also very common in this area. This snake coils to spit a liquid at the eyes of its victim — and is expertly accurate in its aim up to a distance of eight feet. The venom would kill if injected into the blood stream. Although it is not harmful to the skin, if it does get into the eyes it produces a severe burning sensation — at which time the cobra can either retreat to safety or approach and strike its victim, thus injecting the venom through the fangs in the front of the upper jaw. Usually, the snake withdraws, and cases of the follow-up bite are very rare.

There are other poisonous snakes in the area which, unfortunately, are not classified — or, at least, have not been listed in the classifications so far available.[1]

---

[1] Hausa recognises at least eight different poisonous snakes and a similar number of harmless ones, for each of which categories there are some twentyfive different names, varying in use mostly according to area. *(Ed.)*

## B.  MEDICINES.

The following is an attempt at listing the natural or herbal remedies which the Dukkawa employ. In some cases there was a certain discrepancy as to the exact type of plants used, although the part of the plant — e. g. leaves, roots, etc. — was agreed upon, as well as the method of preparation and manner of application. In these instances, the points of unanimity only have been recorded and the names of specific plants when there was any great divergence of opinions has been omitted.

Also recorded is the people's opinions as to the causes of some of the sickness. Though that may have little, if any, medical value, the tone and simplicity of some of these explanations gives an added insight into the general concept of their global society which the Dukkawa enjoy.

*Headache.* Since the people obviously do not have an ability to differentiate between specific types of diseases, any sickness which has a headache as one of its symptoms would be treated as such. The most common cause of a headache, according to informants, is when someone gets hit on the head. Other times headaches 'just happen' for no apparent reason. A few associate headaches as a result of previous excessive social drinking, but this is by no means a universal assumption. One BaDukku, in fact, bought several charms (to be described later in the section on Religion) to protect himself from very severe headaches, which always occured the morning after he had drunk two or three quarts of guinea-corn beer. Though it was suggested that there might be some connection between his drinking and the headaches, he remained convinced that he was being plagued by some evil spirit.

The medicine for headaches is made from the bark of the Frankincense Tree which is pounded and then put into a pot of water. A red-hot rock is put into the water producing a vapor, which is inhaled by the patient who puts a cloth over his head and leans his head over the top of the pot, the cloth falling down far enough to enclose the pot so that no steam escapes.[2]

---

[2] This tree is named *bano* in Hausa. There are two similar types, the Boswellia Dal-

*Stomach ailments.* This general category includes gastric pains, stomach cramps, indigestion, etc. Medicine for these various afflictions is made from the root (not bark) of the *gwandar daji* (wild custard apple, Anona Senegalensis), which is mixed with and stirred into guinea-corn porridge. This porridge is taken three or four times a day.

*Diarrhoea.* Causes of this are held to be the eating of too much fish or the fruit of the mango tree. The remedy for it is made from the bark of a fig tree (*baure* — Ficus Gnaphalocarpa) and the bark of the *taura* tree (Detarium Senegalense). The barks of these two trees are mixed, pounded together and cooked. Then they are stirred into guinea-corn porridge and the mixture is taken three times a day.

*Dysentery.* Sometimes the same medicine prescribed for diarrhoea is used for dysentery also. But there is another type of medicine which is administered in the form of an enema (*guguci*). For this, the bark of the locustbean tree (*dorowa*) is pounded and cooked in water. After it is filtered, it is injected into the rectum through a piece of hollow grass. The medicine is placed in a calabash with a small hole punctured at the base of it — just large enough for the piece of grass to fit through. This hole is 'gummed' on the outside to prevent any leakage. Then the other end of the grass is inserted into the rectum with the patient lying down or bending over.

*Constipation.* The medicine used for this ailment is well known in many parts of Nigeria. The fruit of the[3] *gungwari* tree is peeled and the seeds are removed. The pulp is then pounded and water is added (not cooked), and then a *very small amount* is drunk. This has an almost immediate effect. It is a very powerful medicine and can easily result in

---

zielii, mainly in the area here being considered and the Boswellia Odorata, occurring mainly in the Benue area. *(Ed.)*

[3] As the Author noted, this word can not be found in any reference work as a tree. One hesitates to prescribe at a distance, but there is a sedge grass called *gangawari* which, along with eleven other ingredients is made up into a common aphrodisiac known as *gagayi*. By no stretch of imagination, however, could this be described as a tree. It is possible that the ingredient referred to is the "Physic" or "Purging Nut *(bi ni da zugu)*, Jatropa Curcas, a purgative of such power that its name is a ribald tribute to its effect; "follow me with a floor-cloth." *(Ed.)*

almost uncontrolable motions. Overdoses have in some cases resulted in serious internal ailments.

*Back ache.* The suet of a python is rubbed on the sore spot. The suet is not cooked, just taken and applied.[4]

*Cuts.* The roots of certain plants are dug up and washed (not cooked) and then chewed. The juice is applied to the wound and has a burning sensation — like iodine. In some cases it causes bleeding.

*Tropical ulcers.* These are usually found on the lower extremity of the legs. For the most part, the Dukkawa do not know what causes them, they "just appear". For medication either the bark or the roots of the *kalgo* tree — Bauhinia Reticulata — are used. These are cooked and then a cloth or some dried grass is dipped into the mixture and the sore is washed with the liquid.
Then a piece of bark from the *gwandar daji* — wild custard apple — is peeled and cut to a size that will cover the sore. On top of this is placed a second piece of bark from the *kalgo* tree, both of these are kept in place by a length of Indian hemp or some similar binding which is wrapped around the leg. The medication is applied twice a day, once in the morning and again at night.

*Snake bite.* The roots from any of several trees can be used. One tree is given the general name *uwar magani,*[5] i. e. the Mother of Medicine. Some say the roots should be mixed with onions, others say they never use onions. These roots are pounded and put into cold water, and the water is supposed to be drunk three times a day. The purpose of this is to induce vomitting. The Dukkawa believe that the snake venom will be evacuated in the vomit, thus curing the patient.
Leaves from the *gwandar daji* — wild custard apple — are then warmed near a fire and placed on the site of the snake bite and tied in place.

---

[4] In this area pythons are not numerous, although there are a few. In five years, I have known three of these snakes to have been killed, which tends to suggest that most people bothered by back ache go without 'medical treatment.'

[5] This tree is the *sainya,* Securidaca longipedunculata. Not only is it medicinal, but it also occurs in some prescriptions for arrow poison. Its proper Hausa epithet is *uwar magunguna* (the plural). *(Ed.)*

## CHAPTER SEVEN

# THE FAMILY CIRCLE

## DOMESTIC LIFE

The Dukku tribe, like almost every group in Nigeria, had its own language as well as its own particular customs. In northern Nigeria, the Hausa language is a *lingua franca* which the various tribes use to communicate with each other when they intermingle. But whenever the Dukkawa are among themselves — at home, at *biki,* etc. — they always speak their own language. Since Dukku women seldom leave a completely Dukku environment — except to go to market — many of them understand very little Hausa except for the necessary names of the different kinds of food and other terminology useful in trading. Many of the young children are also under this same restriction. Virtually none of the Dukkawa speak English, although some young men most certainly have the desire.

As indicated previously, the family structure is a simple, patrilinear arrangement. A husband, his wife — or wives — and their children. Larger compounds are based on the same principle: an older man and his wife — or wives — his married sons and their families. In these multi-family compounds, which seldom have more than fifteen adults, everyone lives within the same confines but the compound is divided into sections. The sections are not physically separated, e. g. by fences  or distance, but are just separate parts of the compound where each family has its own group of huts — *d'aki* (personal living quarters), granary, *rumbun mata,* etc. The huts of one brother's family can be next to another brother's, so that to a visitor it would appear as just one large compound. Where there are three or four families living in one compound, one large common guest hut is shared among them. A visitor usually comes to socialize with everyone — or anyone —

and the infrequent travelers encountered are just seeking a place to sleep. A single large guest hut is sufficient for these purposes.

Authority within the compound rests with the father. In compounds where an older man lives with one or more of his married sons, the older man — grandfather — has the general authority over the entire compound and each son has immediate authority within his own family.

Within a family, the senior son holds a special position of respect among the children, even if the eldest child is a girl. When old enough, he has the responsibility of training the other children. If he has an elder sister, she has the right to give him advice, but the boy himself will make the decision. As the senior son matures, the father will more and more refer the making of decisions and the running of the compound to him.

Within a family, the hierarchy of authority is as follows.

1.  Grandfather has authority over the entire compound; father controls his immediate family. In practice, a boy will obey his grandfather in anything pertaining to compound life, whereas in family matters he will obey his father. However, if it should ever happen — as it seldom does — that the grandfather and father disagree, the boy would be expected to follow the command of the grandfather. One can say this 'seldom happens' because compound life is so routine that there are few occasions for discrepancies of opinion.

2.  Father's authority is greater than mother's. It should be pointed out, however, that in general the father trains his sons — with the assistance of the senior son — and the mother trains the daughters. If it should occur that a father and mother disagree concerning the work or duties of one of the daughters, the father's wish would prevail. Again, because of the organization of family life, this just does not happen. First of all, the women are diligent in training their daughters — if for no other reason than it lessens the burden of their own work. This includes such tasks as helping to carry water, gathering firewood, grinding guinea-corn, sweeping the compound, etc. Also, the father is never greatly concerned with these matters. About the only thing that would draw his attention to the fact that the work was not being done properly would be if his food was not prepared on time —

and it has never been known for this to happen! Finally, the understanding within a family is such that if a father expressed his displeasure at anything, his wife would immediately act upon it.

3.    When the father is not present in the compound, the mother's authority may defer to that of the senior son. The senior son's position is primary only in respect to the other children. The mother, as an adult, is given a higher status. This is the case when the senior son is young or in his early teens. If he is married, or of marriageable age, he would be considered mature enough to rule the compound if his father is gone. His mother could give him advice but he himself would make the decision and be accountable to his father for it.

However, since the son would make his decision according to how he thought his father would want it decided — and not according to his personal inclinations — a conflict of opinions between the senior son and his mother is almost inconceiveable since both are familiar with the absent father's likes and dislikes.

The mother's authority — when the senior son is still young — has certain limitations when the father is not home. She herself will not stay away from the compound overnight unless she has previously informed her husband, or if the place she will stay is very close to the compound and the people are well known to — and approved of — by the father. Also, she will not permit any of the children to remain away from the compound overnight unless they will be staying with relatives.

This can cause a serious problem if one of the children happens to need immediate medical attention, e. g. snake bite. Sometimes, even after the urgings of many of the relatives, the woman still refuses to allow the children to be taken from the compound. The relatives may be angry, but they will not act contrary to her decision or attempt to overrule it.

4.    If a man has two wives, the senior wife has the authority when the husband is absent. As pointed out above, since all decisions are determined in regard to the husband's perceived intentions, the senior wife's authority in his absence is seldom a cause of friction between the women.

One regulator of family relationships, whether between the sexes, or between parents and children, or between seniors and juniors is the concept of *kunya* — a word often translated to mean "shame".[1]

By our standards, "shame" ordinarily means a feeling of remorse for having committed some offence or fault. But besides this usage, there is another (perhaps more important) meaning for the word *kunya* among the Dukkawa which has a distinct significance all its own. It would certainly not fully be understood by someone not closely acquaintanted with this culture, and most probably would be subject to complete mis-interpretation.

In this special sense, *kunya* is the reason given for certain abstentions — often most obviously reflected in regard to not speaking someone's name — which arise either from close personal relationships or from a perception that some kind of particular respect is due to be shown to another person.

This can be clearly illustrated by a few examples of the main occasions when it occurs.

1.    A father and mother will be scrupulous in not showing any particular signs of concern for their first born son, whom we have seen to be the only child with any special place within the family. Neither father nor mother will ever speak his name. They will refer to him only as "my first-born son." If they want him to do something, they will usually have one of the other children tell him, or, if they tell him themselves, they will never address him by his name.[2]

---

[1] It is incorrect to translate *kunya* as "shame" except in the loosest of interpretations. *Kunya* really means "modesty" — at least that is probably the nearest the English can arrive at. But *kunya* also has connotations of an "inner voice" prompting an appreciation of what is "proper behaviour" or "respectability" or, in Shakespearean terms, that "modest stillness and humility", than which "nothing so becomes a man" in times of peace.

There is also a strong element of "conscience" in the concept of *kunya*. Fr. Prazan is correct in his belief that long acquaintance with the culture is necessary before it can be fully understood. *(Ed.)*

[2] The late Emir of Yauri, Emir Abdullahi was scrupulous in observing this convention in regard to his eldest son, the present Emir. It is not confined to the Dukkawa and may be said to be general in many parts of West Africa. "Evil Eye" is often given as a basis for it. *(Ed.)*

2.  If the father and son are traveling together — boys seldom travel with their mothers, or any women — and someone inquires about the boy's name, the father will refer the inquirer to someone else — "Ask him". Or the boy might interrupt and answer for himself. If the man is hard-pressed — no one else is present and the boy is not old enough — the parent will usually answer if it is more than just an idle question (e. g. if the child is receiving medicine at a hospital and his name must be known to be recorded).

    There are other ways besides not speaking the first-born son's name that *kunya* is expressed. For example, on one occasion a man's first-born son was bitten by the deadly Carpet Viper snake and the boy was rushed to the hospital. It was the father who called for help but he did not accompany the boy to the hospital. The man's younger brother came to stay with the child.

3.  On another occasion, a young married couple themselves came with their one year old son, but when he died they called a relative to take the child back home for burial and they themselves were not present at the ceremony.

4.  If the only-child is a girl, some of these manifestations of *kunya* will also be shown, but it will not be as strict as for a first born son.

5.  This *kunya* of the father and mother towards their first-born son does not apply to him in reverse (i. e. in regard to him and his parents.) He will use their names in conversation with other people and also in direct address.

6.  When other people are present, a man will not use his wife's name; nor will a woman speak her husband's name. It has not been ascertained whether this is also true if they are alone together — although when two people are alone the direct form of address is seldom used anyway, since it is obvious to whom the speaker is talking.[3]

---

[3] It must, however, be remarked that this convention is not very far removed from the late Georgian or early Victorian custom whereby, as a mark of gentility, a wife addressed her husband as Mr So-and-so, q. v. Dickens' *Dombey and Son* etc. At a lower social level also the habit of reference to a husband by surname only (dropping the Mr. entirely) still survives. Not all Dukku (or Hausa) customs are without their parallels in "Western Civilization"! (Ed.)

7. A man will not speak the names of his wife's parents or of her grandparents; the same is true of a woman in regard to her husband's parents and grandparents. In a later chapter it will be seen that a man usually names his first-born after his father. Since his wife cannot speak his name, she will give the son a second name.

Special joking relationships (Hausa: *abokin wasa*) also exist within the family organization. They too are based on personal relationships, just as *kunya* is, but with an opposite effect. Whereas *kunya* exerts certain prohibitions of expression, the *abokin wasa* relationship is the basis of a greater intimacy in expression than is ordinarily permitted. It provides the occasion when one person — or both parties involved — can joke and exchange mock-insults with the other without any offense being taken.

1. A grandfather enjoys this prerogative with his grandchildren, and — to a limited degree — so do the grandchildren with their grandfather, in as much as they 'go along' with his affections and humor — but not to the extent that they can initiate any of their own.

2. A mutual joking-relationship exists between a man and his brothers-in-law, and a man and his sisters-in-law; similarly, *mutatis mutandis,* a woman and her brothers-in-law and a woman and her sisters-in-law. This relationship becomes very obvious whenever a man and a woman are seen exchanging comments or laughing together, since, in this society, there are fairly well defined lines between men's circles and women's circles which inhibit casual intermingling of the sexes.

3. Just as a grandfather can joke with his grandchildren, he also extends the privilege to the spouses of his grandchildren when they marry.

4. When two men are contemporaries, i. e. they grew up together, a joking-relationship will exist between them and each other's sons. For example: $A$ and $B$ are contemporaries. $A$ is the father of $a$, $B$ is the father of $b$. There will be a joking-relationship between $A$ and $b$, and between $B$ and $a$.

*Punishment.* Because of the overall pattern of Dukku life, children are raised almost completely within the family circle, with very little outside influence. Under constant supervision from the time they are very young, they will grow up well trained in the manner of life that will be expected of them as adults. As a result, offenses – and therefore punishments – are not as frequent as in societies where children are less well attended.

Children will be children, however, in any society and there will always be times when they will be temperamental and refuse to work or use bad language or just be careless. At these times, they are punished. Just as fathers are responsible for the training of their sons, and mothers for their daughters, so too are punishments meted out from these respective sources.

Since the job of training the children is delegated to the senior son when he is mature enough, he sometimes assumes this more onerous task as well in regard to his younger brothers. He will never, however, physically inflict punishment on one of his sisters. This is left either to the mother or the senior daughter.

Corporal punishment is rare among the Dukkawa. When it does occur, it is usually with small children – playing close to the fire or touching some breakable object – more as a warning than a punishment. When corporal punishment is administered, it is either by hand or with a small stick. A much more common punishment is to give the child some added work to do, and, for a more serious offense, making it go without a meal.

A psychological punishment (regarded as being severe) is to send the child away to the compound of a relative, who, in turn, gives him a good 'talking to' and then returns home with him and tells the parents that "He promises never to do it again." If it happens that the child ever *does* do it again, he then has the relative to worry about as well as his parents![4]

*Inheritance.* In general, if the father dies, the eldest son inherits. Strictly speaking, the wife gets nothing although the eldest son will provide for her. If the mother dies, the eldest daughter has

---

[4] In many societies this is a role that falls to the mother's brother, the maternal uncle. Since he has special responsibilities towards the children of his sister, it would be almost unthinkable for a child to "let him down". The disciplinary bonds of such relationships are enormously strong. *(Ed.)*

a similar role and responsibility. In the first case, the eldest son will usually share the inheritance with his younger brothers according to his discretion — none of them has any proper claim to anything. The same applies in the case of an eldest daughter who inherits from her mother.

If one of the sons dies, two courses seem to apply. The father may either take his dead son's things and redistribute them among the remaining sons, or they may all go to the senior son.

**CHAPTER EIGHT**

# DAILY ROUTINE

A.   GENERAL DESCRIPTION.

Before considering the daily routine of Dukku life, it should again be called to mind how much the seasonal changes influence the pattern of living. For approximately one half of the year the men are occupied with farming and nothing else. Then for the other half of the year there is absolutely no farming at all. It is at this time that other things intrude into their lives, such as repairing their compounds, hunting, etc.

The women's lives follow a more fixed or regular pattern throughout the year, but even their activities are to some extent affected by seasonal changes — the most notable being their pre-occupation with gathering sheanuts and the making of oil from them during the months of June to August.

Dukku daily routine thus lacks any real continuity which can be said to pervade throughout the three hundred and sixty-five days a year. It is good always to bear this in mind lest a too rigid concept be formed of the daily activities. Nonetheless, extrapolating from these variations, there *is* a certain continuity of activity which can be outlined.

*Morning.* The Dukkawa rise with the sun. Some — usually women — are even up before this, rising as soon as the sky turns grey with the coming dawn. A woman's first task of the day is to take the water pots and go to the nearest stream or pool. At the water they will first bathe, and then dip water to be brought back to the compound where it will be poured into the large water containers. Depending on the time of the year — when water is more or less available, and people are more or less thirsty — women will make from three to five trips a day to fetch water.

After returning with the water, the women will scour the cooking pots with guinea-corn stalks and start to boil water which will later be used for cooking. Afterwards they will either sweep the compound or immediately enter the kitchen hut — to begin grinding guinea-corn into meal for *tuwo*. If the women are hungry during the morning, they will eat cold *tuwo* which has been stored away from the previous night's meal.

When it is sheanut season, the women usually get up even earlier to go and bathe and bring water. After that, the remainder of the morning will be spent in the bush gathering nuts. Grinding the guinea-corn for cooking will have been done the evening before.

Men after rising, will usually wash in the compound, dipping water from the water container with a calabash. They will wait until later in the morning to bathe at the stream, and, during the farming season, they will not bathe until the day's work is done.

If it is the farming season, a man will then go immediately to the farm. If the farm is adjacent to the compound, or very close to it, he will return around nine o'clock for some cold *tuwo* and then go back to the farm until mid-day. If the farm is more than a mile away, he will either eat the *tuwo* before he leaves the compound in the morning, or he will take some with him to eat at the farm.

If it is not the farming season, after washing, the men will work on compound repairs or rebuilding. If it is the hot season, when the compound repairs have been already taken care of, and the men have not gone on a hunting trip that year, they will most likely be found just sitting in the shade.[1] About eleven o'clock, or sometime before the sun hits its noonday peak, men will go to bathe.

During the morning hours, young girls will help the women, especially with grinding guinea-corn and sweeping the compound. Six and seven year old girls commonly assist with these chores. When they are older, and stronger, they will help bring water also.

---

[1] This reminds one of the Hausa proverb: *Bawan damuna, tajirin rani* i. e. 'a slave during the Rainy Season becomes the master during the Hot Season.' For half of the year the Dukkawa are 'slaving' on their farms, and for the other half their lives are ones of comparative leisure. (Editorial Note: It must be pointed out that the proverb in question could also be translated "Be a slave (i. e. work like one) in the growing season and you will be a rich man at the end of it!" The author's interpretation is, however, not too far fetched. Hausa Proverbs are intended to be given multiple interpretations.)

Sometimes they are sent to bush to gather different types of leaves which are used for making *miya*.

Younger boys — six and seven years old — are usually delegated to take care of any sheep and goats that the family has. They can also feed the chickens and guinea fowl, bring extra firewood, lend anyone — man or woman — a helping hand, and they are always available for running errands. When they are nine or ten years old they tend the cattle, if the family happens to have any. This is done for about three hours in the morning, and the same length of time in the evening.

*Afternoon.* About twelve o'clock, the women will start to cook. This meal will be the first cooked meal of the day. Guinea-corn meal will be mixed into boiling water to make *tuwo,* and vegetables, often in the form of leaves, and small pieces of meat or fish form the base of the *miya* which is made separately to be eaten with it. Various types of seasoning will be added to this.

If the men have not been in the compound during the morning, they will have come back by noontime. The few whose farms are some miles from their compounds, will have taken guinea-corn meal with them when they left in the morning. A moderate amount of this added to boiling water produces a thick gruel — *kunu* — which can be drunk or eaten with a spoon. Rather than return the two or three miles to their compounds for the noonday meal, such farmers will boil water at the farm and have their gruel.

The mid-day meal is eaten about one o'clock, after which the people relax until three or four o'clock in the afternoon. If anybody does any work during this time of day, it is the type of work which can be done sitting down in a shady area. Some people may take a nap, but most of them just sit and talk.

About three o'clock, or thereabouts, people begin to stir again. Men will go back to their farms, or continue the work they were doing around the compound. Boys will check the goats and sheep, or return to where the cattle are grazing. If wood is needed, the women will go to collect it, after which they will take the pots to the stream to bring water. Many of the women will take the opportunity to bathe again while at the stream. Returning to the compound they will again sweep it out and continue with any small tasks they had been working on.

*Late evening.* As the sun goes down, about seven o'clock, the men will return from their farms or stop doing their work around the compound. Boys will return from tending the sheep or goats or the cattle. Sunset is the sign for the women to start thinking about preparing the evening meal. They will start heating the water and preparing the different ingredients which will go into the *miya*.

Since the day's work is finished for the men and boys, they go to the stream to bathe, after which they return to the compound and relax until it is time to eat.

About eight-thirty or nine o'clock the food is served: the *tuwo* in calabash bowls and the *miya* in the clay ones. When the meal is finished, the women will wash the utensils and store away any of the remaining *tuwo* to be eaten the following morning. This is the last item on the work schedule for the day. For about an hour afterwards the men and women — in separate groups — will sit and talk, and one by one they will move off to go to sleep. By ten-thirty most people have retired for the night.

## B.   SPECIFIC ASPECTS OF ROUTINE.

There are particular aspects of any society's daily routine which, no matter how varied the schedule, are always present, such as cooking and eating, sleeping, and washing. These are the necessary elements of life common to all in every part of the globe. But, because of this universality, they offer excellent opportunities for analysis and comparison since they can be seen not only for the intrinsic value that each activity has in itself but also, by the relation of it to the manner in which other people respond to similar necessities, comparisons between societies can be clearly drawn.

But besides the three activites mentioned above, cooking and eating, sleeping, and washing (hygiene) — there is one further aspect of Dukku life which deserves special mention. In everyday language this could well be described as *common courtesy*. Although there is no special time or place that can be assigned to it in the daily schedule, greetings and displays of deference are essential aspects of daily inter-relationship. Such common courtesies can also be considered to be manifested in particular forms as extensions of the obligation of hospitality.[2]

Cooking.

The place where the cooking is done is very simply arranged. It is always outside (during the Rainy Season, if it happens to be raining at the time the cooking is necessary, an improvised place can be made inside the kitchen hut). A small hole is dug, not more than six inches deep and about twelve to fifteen inches in diameter, and large stones are placed around the circumference. The pot in which the *tuwo* will be cooked is cradled on top of the stones. A smaller "burner" about eight or ten inches in diameter, is fashioned in the same way. The *miya* will be cooked in a smaller pot on top of these stones. (See Figs. 22 and 23).

As mentioned in an earlier chapter, *tuwo* can be made from either guinea-corn, millet, or rice. Although rice can be purchased in some of the marketplaces, the Dukkawa themselves do not grow it, and no example of them eating *tuwon shinkafa* — porridge made from rice — has been observed. For all practical purposes, it is safe to say that guinea-corn *tuwo* is the only kind eaten by the Dukkawa — remembering, however, that millet will be used as an emergency substitute if — and only if — the previous year's guinea-corn fails before the new harvest comes in.

A general description of *tuwo* has already been given, but the full preparation process — from the grain to the prepared food — is as follows.

A bundle of guinea-corn is removed from the granary,[3] the bundle is untied and the stalks are then beaten with a stick until

---

[2] It is refreshing indeed to see this essential "deference" so forthrightly described. Only too often it has been sadly misinterpreted by scholars, who have read into it *(inter alia)* fear, opression, patronage, clientage, slavishness and cowardice. It is nice to see it described just as what it really is, *common courtesy.* It does, however, still have within it a recognition of the basic element of social or community living — social discipline — whether exercised within the context of a wolf pack, a troop of baboons or human communities! *(Ed.)*

[3] At the time of the harvest, twenty or more stalks of guineacorn are laid across lengths of grass rope something over a yard long. The stalks are all laid with their heads pointing in opposite directions so that the bare stalks are all towards the middle. When enough stalks are laid, the rope is tied and the resultant tight bundle *(dami)* is then stored with the others in the granary. *(Ed.)*

all the grain is separated from them. It is then scooped together
in a calabash and taken to the kitchen hut where it is husked. After the husking, it is taken outside and winnowed. Two calabashes
are used for this. The calabash with the guinea-corn is held above
the head; an empty calabash is held about three feet beneath the
elevated one, and the guinea-corn is poured from one into the other.
This is done several times, the wind blowing away the bran, after
which the cracked grain is ground a second time. The guinea-corn
meal is now ready for cooking.

A small amount (it is not all cooked at the same time) of the
meal is mixed with cold water and cooked for fifteen or twenty
minutes. This is a very thin mixture since much more water was
used then meal. Once this initial portion is held to be cooked, additional guinea-corn is added, little by little, the whole always being stirred with a stick lest it cling to the side of the pot and burn.
More and more guinea-corn is added until the desired thickness is
achieved. This process takes about fifteen minutes, depending
upon the amount of food that will be needed.

When the final guinea-corn had been added and stirred thoroughly into the mixture the pot is covered with a clay lid and the
whole is allowed to continue cooking for another five or ten minutes — so that the last guinea-corn to be added will be properly
cooked. The fire is then quenched and the *tuwo* is allowed to cool
for about ten or fifteen minutes, after which it is scooped out into
calabashes, depending upon how many people will be eating. This
entire process is not followed everytime a woman wants to cook a
meal! She will ordinarily beat, grind, and winnow enough guinea-
corn to last two or three days.

As can be imagined, *tuwo* is very bland, being nothing more
than corn and water. There are no spices or condiments used in its
preparation, not even salt. But *tuwo* is not eaten alone, it is eaten
together with *miya* — sauce gravy. A ball of tuwo, fashioned in the
fingers, is dipped into the thick gravy and then eaten.

Various types of seasoning are employed in the *miya*. The
base of the *miya* can be prepared from either meat, fish, or from
vegetables. Since the Dukkawa are not fishermen, the fish they use
for *miya* is purchased in the marketplace. The Dukkawa raise domestic animals, as well as being hunters of wild game, so in most

cases they provide their own meat, although, on account of some particular customs, everyone does not always eat it — as will be pointed out shortly.

The vegetables which are used as a base for their *miya* are those which they either grow themselves or which grow wild in the bush. A few things — like onions (if they choose to use them), peppers, and salt — will have to be bought.

The following is a listing of the various types of plants, and parts of plants, which are used in making *miya*.

1.  Leaves from the baobab tree. (Hausa *kuka*)
2.  The inner substance of the baobab tree pod. (Hausa *garin kuka*)
3.  Okra. (Hausa *kub'ewa*)
4.  Squash (which is cut up in small pieces) (Hausa *kabewa*), (Cucurbit Peto and C. Maxima.)
5.  Leaves of the Red Sorrel (Hausa *yakuwa*) (Hibiscus Sabdariffa)
6.  Locustbeans (Hausa *dorawa*)
7.  Leaves of the *yaud'o* — a herb (Ceratotheca Sesamoides)
8.  Leaves of the Indian hemp (Hausa *rama*)

Sometimes these things are used as the main ingredient in the *miya*, e. g. okra and locustbeans — but usually they are used to season fish or meat.

The meat used in the preparation of *miya*, involves some customs peculiar to the Dukkawa. This is only in regard to Dukku women. Men will eat any kind of the meat which is commonly acceptable to all people in this area — although they ordinarily do not eat dog, which is eaten as a delicacy by the Kamberi and Gungawa.

In general, however, Dukku women will not eat *any kind* of meat from the time they start to develop breasts until after they are married — i. e. from about twelve to sixteen years of age. This is not a hard and fast rule, but more or less applies as a general one. For example, some girls do not eat meat from the time they are six or seven years old.

Even after marriage, there are some restrictions which women observe about meat. Most women will never eat the meat of a domestic animal, such as a cow, goat, chicken etc. Again, however, this is a generalization, and the strict observation of this restriction varies from area to area. Women will, however, eat the meat of game animals: warthogs, duiker, gazelle, hares, bush rats, monkeys, and even snakes. There does seem to be an exception made in the case of older women who will eat meat of any kind. The *miya*, whatever kind is prepared, is usually made with sheanut oil. Sometimes the oil from peanuts is used.

This combination of *tuwo* and *miya* is cooked twice a day, once at noontime, and again for the evening meal, between about eight or nine o'clock. These are the second and third meals which the Dukkawa eat during the day. The first meal — which is more like a snack than a meal (cold *tuwo* without any *miya*) — is eaten in the early morning. If there is not any *tuwo* remaining from the previous night, guinea-corn gruel — *kunu* — will be made for this morning meal.

When there are several families living within the same compound, the women will rotate the cooking chores. One woman will cook one meal, another woman will cook the next. There is no deferential treatment as far as food is concerned, no special food for individuals. Everybody eats the *tuwo* and *miya* that is prepared.

Eating.

Men and women never eat together. The men eat in groups of two or three (from one bowl of *tuwo* and one bowl of *miya*) and the women arrange themselves in the same way. Even when there is only one man and one woman living in a compound, they will not eat together. The groups of two and three usually separate according to age groups. Young boys will eat with the older men; young girls with the older women. Older boys will eat with the men; older girls with the women.

When the food is brought, a calabash of water is also brought. This is used to wash the hands and to rinse out the mouth; most men — and some women — chew kola nuts at some time during the day; some also chew tobacco. The food is always eaten with the right hand (the left hand is for sanitary purposes). When the meal is finished, the mouth is again rinsed, and the teeth are 'brushed' with the fingers.

One of the girls will then gather up any left-overs, which, in the case of *tuwo* will be put into one calabash and then stored away.

Sleeping.

Husband and wife always sleep together in the same hut. In the cases when a BaDukku has more than one wife, each wife usually has her own hut and some agreement is made as to sleeping arrangements (one or two nights with each wife). The husband sleeps on a mud bed and his wife sleeps on the floor. Both lie on grass mats.

During the Hot Season, everyone sleeps outside, at least until the early hours of the morning. At this time, the men sleep in one section of the compound and the women sleep in another. When sleeping indoors, the people sleep naked, unless it is the cool Harmattan Season. But when sleeping outdoors, they always cover their loins. This may sound obvious, but women of the Kamberi tribe sometimes sleep naked when they sleep outdoors.

Children sleep with their parents until they reach six or seven years of age when they will sleep with their older brothers and sisters. There is one hut where the older boys and unmarried men sleep; another hut for the older girls. If a child has no older brothers — or sisters, as the case may be — a hut will be built when he is old enough to sleep alone. A boy is about eight years old when this is acknowledged; if a girl is to sleep alone, her separate sleeping hut is not constructed until she is older, about ten years of age. In a compound where there is only one older child, he — or she — might sleep in a near-by compound where there are older children, rather then having to have a special hut built.

Hygiene.

*Bodily Cleanliness.* As has been pointed out, in general, Dukkawa bathe twice a day. The women bathe the first thing in the morning, when they go to fetch water, and again in the late afternoon when they usually go for water again before sweeping the compound and beginning preparations for the evening meal. Men will bathe later in the morning (unless they are on the farm, in which case it would be senseless to bathe and then immediately return to the farm work for the day) and again in the evening when they return from farming or have finished the day's work around the compound.

This is the general pattern which, naturally, is susceptible to variation. Besides ordinary circumstances which might occasionally prevent a person from going to the stream to bathe, the principal difficulty in this regard is an insufficiency of available water. This is a very real problem, for bathing, and, much more so, for drinking and cooking water, during the last months of the Hot Season (April and May).

The previous year's rains ended in October, which means there has not been any rainfall for six months. Immediately after the Rainy Season, the sandy ravine beds are saturated with moisture and water collects in them, but this gradually diminishes as the weeks pass by. By the first of the year there are only a few pools of water scattered here and there throughout the bush.

As soon as these also dry up, the women have to start digging (with their hands) in the sand of the dry stream beds to reach water. At first this is not difficult; water will be obtained within six inches from the surface. But as the weeks pass by, and the beginning of the Hot Season approaches in early March, the digging goes deeper and deeper. Sometimes it may go more than three feet deep before a particular stream bed has to be abandoned as of no further use, and the women have to move further away from the compound in search of water.

During the latter part of the Hot Season, water is rationed very carefully. The first consideration is water for cooking, then for drinking, and finally, water for bathing. People will use water very sparingly for bathing, dipping a calabash full − or sufficiently full − of water, and going to a secluded place inside, or outside, the compound to wash. As water becomes still more scarce, this kind of bathing will just be performed once a day − in the evening before the meal. Washing from a calabash will also be done during other times of the year when a person does not have the opportunity to go to stream.

There are no designated places for bathing. A person − man or woman − (or groups of men, or groups of women) − will go to the closest place where there is water.

The Dukkawa always use soap when bathing. Although they themselves do not make soap (which can be made very readily from sheabutter), it is available in all of the marketplaces. After washing they rub pomade over their bodies and into their hair. This pomade, which is used by both men and women, costs one shilling and six pence for a jar that will last about two weeks. — Some tribes will use pomade, or some scented liquid, when they have not had a chance to bathe — as a quick substitute. The Dukkawa only use pomade after having bathed properly.

After pomade is massaged into the scalp, the hair is combed (a comb costs from four to six pence). People have their hair cut once every two to three months, the hair being completely removed at this time. Razorblades, which can be purchased cheaply in the market, are used for this. Years ago — before the advent of the razorblade — blacksmiths forged triangular pieces of thin metal (about three inches long) which were sharpened on one side and used for haircutting and shaving. But this is a product of by-gone days since razorblades are both sharper and cheaper.

Before the hair is cut, the head is washed with cold water (sometimes soap is used). After the cutting, the head is again washed. Some people — both men and women — will rub charcoal on their heads until the hair starts to come out again.

Men are shaved — they never shave themselves — about once a month. The shaving is done in the same manner as haircutting. As for the actual barbering, anyone can do it. Therefore, a woman could shave a man, a man could cut a woman's hair, a girl could cut a man's hair, etc. etc. Fingernails are cleaned with a thin stick and trimmed with a razorblade or sharp knife. Toenails are also trimmed in this way.

*Bodily functions.* There is no special area or place designated for this. Any secluded spot, at least fifty yards from the compound, is sufficient. Men will sometimes urinate closer to the compound, but this is not the custom. No Dukku compound has ever been visited in which any person has urinated within the confines of the compound, nor do the Dukkawa themselves admit the possibility of such a thing happening, but it has been noted among some other tribes.

*Clothes,* especially the better ones which are worn to market or to *biki,* are washed fairly regularly. Although the clothes are simple, usually just a piece of cloth, they are almost invariably clean whenever a BaDukku is in public (e. g. at market or a *biki*). Cloth is washed with soap and water, and is then placed on a rock and beaten with the hand. Loinclothes are cleaned first by soaking them in hot water, drying them, and then rubbing butter *(man shanu)* on them. Ordinarily, everyone washes his own clothes, although sometimes a woman will wash her husband's and vice versa.

A few Dukkawa filter their *drinking water* through a piece of cloth but this is not a general practice.[4] The Dukkawa do not boil their drinking water. It is drunk just as it is brought from the stream or pool.

There is no special place for *rubbish,* it is just disposed of in the bush. However, the Dukkawa exercise such stringent economy that almost everything that can be used in one way or another, is, so that there really is very little that can be described as rubbish. It is not a problem of disposing of tin cans and bottles — they are valuable!

Greetings.

The following are descriptions of greetings as they are exchanged between two Dukku people. Such exchanges can be ob-

---

[4] The Editor is fascinated by this observation! During the 1940's the then Colonial Government made strenuous efforts to eradicate *kurkunu* — Guineaworm (Filaria Medinensis).

The campaign included extensive rebuilding of existing wells and the sinking of thousands of new ones. It was spectacularly successful in town and village situations, but it was realised from the beginning that in societies like the Dukkawa, special difficulties presented themselves. However, the Guineaworm's eggs, though small, are capable of separation from water by a rough filter such as is here described. In such cases therefore every opportunity was taken to urge groups like the Dukkawa to pass their drinking water through squares of rough calico (technically "grey baft") and the Editor as a young Cadet in Yauri Emirate spent much time explaining the system, and, Government parsimony being notorious, spending his own money on bolts of baft to cut up into squares for free distribution. That this practice still survives is heartening. That it was successful would seem to be borne out by the fact that there is no mention of Guineaworm (or of its treatment) in the text, in spite of its wide prevalence a generation ago. The appearance of the practice recorded as "Dukku custom", does, however, give cause for thought in connection with the ease which "custom" can be "incubated." *(Ed.)*

served quite commonly when two people meet while travelling or
when someone enters a compound.

When entering a compound where there are several men,
ordinarily only the master of the house will receive the full
formal greeting, the other men merely being verbally greeted.
An exception would be if another man present were to be an
elder, in which case he too would be given the full respectful
greeting.
When a BaDukku is greeting a non-Dukkawa, the forms of
greeting may, or may not, be slightly modified (but always
the full greeting is awarded to anyone of any tribe who is
considered to be an elder or to hold some special authority).

1.  When two men meet, they will each make a very slight
    bow to each other and exchange verbal greetings.

2.  If a man meets an elder, he will remove his cap and his
    sandals. Then he will squat down as the verbal greetings
    are made. In his turn, the elder will usually also remove
    his cap although ordinarily he will not remove his sandals.
    Nor does the elder squat down during the greeting-ex-
    change. The removal of one's sandals is an ubiquitous sign
    of respect throughout northern Nigeria. It is done before
    entering a host's compound, before entering a guest hut
    (if you are a guest and have been invited inside), and on
    other similar occasions.

3.  When two elders meet, they will each tip their caps to
    the back of their heads, but will not completely remove
    them. They will then make very slight bows to each other,
    but neither will squat down. Nor will either remove his
    shoes.

4.  A man will merely verbally greet a woman, there will be
    no physical gestures. On the woman's part, she will make
    a slight bow to the man. Greetings between a man and a
    woman are not as prolonged as between two men; just an
    exchange of three or four phrases, before they pass their
    separate ways. Men and women in fact really do not have
    much in common to talk about when they meet, except
    maybe to inquire as to the where-abouts of a certain
    person. Men have no particular interest in woman's activi-

ties, and vice versa. A woman would hardly ask "How is the farming?" If it does happen that a conversation ensues, it is always direct and to the point. If a man meets an elderly woman, he will probably make a differential bow, which she will return.

5. Women simply exchange verbal greetings with each other.

The handshake, as a form of greeting, is foreign to this culture. But it has been adopted by Nigerians who have been exposed to western customs, and now even a few Dukkawa use this form of greeting, though it is not a widespread practice. However, a Dukku man will never seek to shake hands with a woman.

*Hospitality.* When a person approaches someone's compound he will call out a greeting. Sometimes he will use the standard greeting which is universal in Hausaland — *salamu alaikun* (peace to you) — to which the standard response is the same greeting in reverse — *alaikun salamu.* It is noteworthy that if the response is not returned from inside the compound, the visitor — even a close friend — will not enter.

A response to the greeting constitutes an invitation for the visitor to enter the compound. The master of the house — or whoever is in authority at the time — will bring a mat for him to sit on, which is either placed inside the guest hut or outside in some convenient place. Then water will be offered.

It must be remembered that visitors such as this are always men. A woman's life — except for going to market and going to bush for wood and water — is strictly centered within the compound. If she has to visit someone during the daytime, most likely the men will not be home anyway. If it happens that they are, there is a brief greeting and she goes about what she came for. Women will not be visiting anyone in the evening; it is the time of cooking for their families.

After water is offered to the visitor, he will be invited to eat if it is mealtime, or near to it. Otherwise, cold *tuwo* or some kind of food will be offered. The visitor will exchange greetings with everyone in the compound, even the women, but after that his main conversation will be carried on with the master of the house and with any other men who choose to come and participate.

If the master of the house, or some adult male, is not at home, the wife will stand just inside the compound and greet the visitor, but he will not be invited to enter (nor would he think of doing so). If it so happens that he asks for food, he will not be refused. He will be asked to enter the guest hut and a mat will be brought for him to sit on. This constitutes the one exception to the ban on entering the compound, since it would be considered a greater offense to refuse food to a person. However, most guest huts are situated in such a way that they are located at the entrance to the compound. In many instances, the cornstalk fence which surrounds the compound is built to the sides of the guest hut so that a person must walk through the guest hut in order to pass beyond the fence (Fig. 35). When the visitor finishes eating, he will leave immediately. Under no circumstances — unless the man is an intimate friend of the master would he be permitted to stay overnight in the compound.

If the master is home, anybody wishing to sleep overnight in the compound will usually be able to do so. The only person who will be refused would be a mad man, for fear that he might harm the children. Lepers will not be refused nor will non-Dukku "strangers". In fact, many times they are encouraged to stay. Once a person is admitted into the compound, he is treated as one of the family — and even better. Whatever little the Dukkawa have to offer — food, if there is any, beer, tobacco, kolanuts, etc., — all will be offered to the visitor.

As is frequently the case throughout the world, people who have the least always seem to go to the greatest lengths to share what little they have.

Just as there was a natural transition to be observed from the communality of a settlement's to the privacy and individuality of a home's domestic routine, so now there is a similar transition to be remarked between the purely physical and material aspects of Dukku home life and the climacterics around which, in common with the rest of humanity, these all tend to revolve — birth, adolescence (or puberty, which in so many tribal cultures center around initiation ceremonies at this time), marriages and death.

In the Dukku culture, however, there are no initiation rites

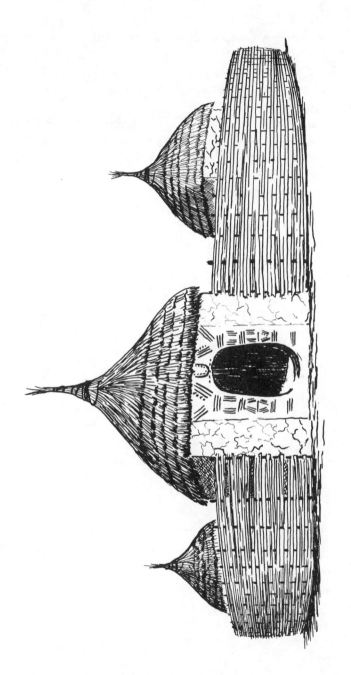

Fig. 35. Sketch of a typical compound, showing the entrance hut (*zaure*) as the focal point.

or ceremonies, or, indeed, any other significant events at all, which are associated with adolescence, and therefore no consideration of this particular phase of life will be necessary in this study.

The three remaining milestones in the life cycle, birth, marriage and death will now each be dealt with separately in the following three chapters.

One point must here be clarified. *Biki* are associated both with marriage and with death. They are also associated with many other social events. Since any consideration of them amounts more to of a description of the ceremonies involved rather than an outline of the moral or social considerations pertaining to the events which led up to them, the *biki* themselves will be discussed separately in a further chapter.

However, any elements which have relevance to the overall beliefs and practices concerning those for marriage or for death will be referred to in their appropriate places.

## CHAPTER NINE

# LIFE-CYCLE: BIRTH

The Dukkawa are generally ignorant of any precise details of why a woman actually conceives. Indeed, they appear to be rather mystified by the whole matter. They say — almost to a man — that they sleep with their wives in the same way all the time, and sometimes that the women conceive and sometimes they do not! And, they add, for some reason, some women conceive more frequently than others. Then again, some women conceive at more or less regular intervals, say, within a year after giving birth, while other women conceive irregularly, e. g. one year after the previous birth, then three years, then a year and a half, etc.

The universal solution to these variations which is offered is "They conceive when God wants them to conceive."

"God's will" is, indeed, the catch-all answer to any question which seems insoluble. In some cases it may be quite inconsequential, but at other times it is often pathetically relevant — as when a person who is seriously sick is not brought for proper medical treatment, and dies: the people will simply say that "God wanted him to die." Fortunately, this attitude is rapidly diminishing.[1]

Besides the irregular patterns of conception, noted above there are, of course always cases when a woman never conceives at all. There is a traditional medicine which can be given, but in cases

---

[1] Unlike Father Prazan, some observers have read into this innate "fatalism" less complimentary attitudes such as callousness, apathy and dis-interest. But, in a society that does not believe (rightly or wrongly) that it has a technological competence capable of controlling most, or at least much, catastrophe, whether personal or social, "God's Will" remains a powerful rationalisation for disaster. It has been so for generations in Western Civilization, when societies were simpler and the world was less sure of itself. (Ed.)

like this, the woman is immediately suspected of and will first be interrogated in regard to possible acts of adultery. If no accusation can be supported then the medicine will be administered. This medicine is made from the leaves of certain trees, which are infused in water which is then given to the woman to drink. Not all Dukkawa are familiar with it, and sometimes someone from outside the immediate family will have to be called in to make it — but not until the necessary preliminary interrogations have been undertaken by the elders within the family circle. If a woman still does not conceive after taking the medicine, it is presumed that the failing is due either to a sin of her mother, or to a curse put on her by one of her parents.

If a man is impotent, he is not subject to interrogation. He himself may try medicines, or charms. In contrast to the case of a woman who has been interrogated and has proven her fidelity, in the case of continued impotence in a man, he himself will be suspected of some sin (whereas a woman's condition will be traced back, in some way to her parents). One possible reason for this attribution of culpability could be the comparative certainty in ascertaining the activities of a woman (which are very restricted) against those of a man who has the freedom of movement to go wherever, and whenever, he wants.

A woman will usually wait two or three months before telling her husband she is pregnant. Intercourse will continue between them until the sixth or seventh month of her pregnancy.

When the time comes for delivery, the place where the birth will occur is the woman's hut. As will be pointed out in the next chapter on marriage customs, it is the practice of the Dukkawa that the wife will remain living in her parent's compound until sometime after the first child is born. Sometime after this she will then move to live permanently with her husband, either in the compound of her husband's family, or in a distinct compound which the husband has built for them. A first child, therefore, is born in the girl's private hut in her parent's compound. This will always be the case, even in those instances when the girl moves in with her husband before the first birth. When the time comes for delivery, she will return to her parent's compound, but only for the first child.

The only preparation in the hut is a fire which will continually burn during the delivery and afterwards until the new mother leaves it, which can be either three or four days after delivery.[2] The doorway of the hut will be closed and no one except the woman, or women, who assist with the delivery will be permitted to enter. For the days that this takes place the husband will most likely leave the compound and stay with a friend. Here, again, the concept of *kunya* enters in.

When a woman is very close to her time she will be given a drink to facilitate the process. This drink is made from the bark of a special tree, which is pounded, and then mixed with potash in water. Any older woman can act as midwife. For the first child, if the mother of the girl's father (paternal grandmother) is able, she will always be the midwife, the actual birth taking place in the compound of the girl's parents.

The midwife's role is one of compassionate assistance during the time that the labor-pains are increasing. She will warm her hands near the fire, and press them against the woman's breasts and stomach as a means of soothing the pain. It does not appear that pressing the hands on the stomach is intended in any way physically to assist the delivery of the baby.

As the pains develop and become more frequent, the woman is lying on her back. However, when the birth seems imminent, the ordinary position for delivery is a kneeling one.

When the baby is born, the umbilical cord is measured to the baby's knee and is then cut with a sharp knife or razorblade. The remaining cord is put into a clay pot and buried, either within the woman's hut or just outside the doorway.[3] The midwife will then wash the woman's body with warm water into which some leaves have been mixed. The custom of some tribes — not the Dukkawa — is to wash the woman with very hot water which is almost scalding,

---

[2] The belief in heat in the hut at the time of a birth is not limited to the Dukkawa. It is very widespread indeed, and in the Hausa culture there is very little doubt of its efficacy both for easing the birth itself and for speeding the mother's return to full activity. *(Ed.)*

[3] It is interesting to note that there appears to be none of the excessive concern for the secret disposal of the after-birth which characterizes many of the sub-cultures in Hausaland, including that of the Hausa themselves. *(Ed.)*

sometimes actually burning the skin. After the washing, the woman is rubbed with oil. Sometimes this is sheanut oil, sometimes it is a special oil made from the roots of a tree which have an orange color. The baby will also be washed and rubbed with the same oil.

If the woman has given birth to a son, she will remain confined in her hut for three days; if a daughter has been born, she will remain for four days. During this time of enclosure, a special kind of soup will be made for the woman which she will drink three times a day. It is made from fish and cornstalk ashes are added to it. The reason for ashes is said to be to 'clean the stomach'. There is no specific explanation given as to how the ashes clean the stomach, except that this is what was told to people by their parents.

If a woman has prolonged labor pains and is having difficulty with the delivery, she is given medicine to drink. The medicine is made from the roots of the *yaud'on daji* herb (Ceratotheca sesamoids) which are pounded and cooked. If the baby is delivered, but the placenta is not expelled, another kind of medicine is made from the bark of the African Rosewood tree *madobia*.[4] The bark is pounded and cooked in water, and the woman drinks this.

If a child is born dead, the woman is washed and rubbed with oil. The special soup is not prepared for her (which is remarkable since the purpose of the soup is to 'clean the stomach' which would seem to be necessary regardless of whether the child was born dead or alive). As a period of mourning, among some of the Dukkawa, the would-be mother will not do any work for a few days; among others there is no mourning period or any other external signs of grief. The child is merely buried and nobody refers to the incident any further.

Although it is not a strict custom, a new mother might receive some fish as a gift for her first-born child (but not for any following births), which would usually be given by one of the grandfathers of the child.

Twins are considered a special blessing. Although there is no particular ceremony, there is a custom that the maternal grand-

---

[4] Pterocarpus Erinaceus. The blood-red resin from the trunk of this tree is a variety of "African Kino" or "Dragons Blood", a medicinal astringent. *(Ed.)*

father of the children buys a large piece of cloth which is divided into two equal pieces, one being given to each of the children.

As mentioned earlier, a woman will remain in her hut for three days after giving birth to a son, for four days after giving birth to a daughter. On the day that she comes out, the name will be given to the child. There is no strict rule as to who names the children, although if the first-born child is a boy, it often happens that the maternal grandfather of the boy gives him his name. Other than that, each family decides the way in which the children will be named. In some families, the father names all the children; in other families the father names the boys and the mother names the girls. This is in regard to the first name of the child, since — for various reasons — a child will usually have more than one name.

There are two cases when it is necessary to give a second name. A father will usually name one of his sons after his own father (if he himself names the first son, this will usually be the case; if the maternal grandfather of the boy names him, then the father will name his second son after *his* father).

A mother, however, cannot say this name, so she will perforce have to give the boy a second one. And since the child in his earliest years will be almost completely associated with his mother, this second name will be the one which people will commonly hear, and which, naturally, he will become known by it as he grows up.

The second case is a similar instance, i. e. if the mother names one of her daughters after her own mother — a name which the child's father cannot speak. The father will then give the girl a second name by which he can call her.

It may happen also that someone might add a third, and even a fourth name. This could be any of the grandparents of the child, older brothers or sisters of either the mother or father, or even someone outside the compound — or, occasionally, a non—Dukkawa. Sometimes a person remarks on a characteristic of the child, and this name catches on. For example, a Fulani man was visiting a Dukkawa compound and saw a new-born boy. He remarked that he was a large child and that he would grow up to be a hard worker — *bawa* — at farm work. The people in the compound re-

marked on the man's comment, and from that day the boy was
called *Bawa*.[5]

Unlike many other tribes — e. g. Hausa, Yoruba, and Ibo —
there is no naming ceremony for which people are invited and a
feast is prepared. On the day when the woman comes out of her
hut, either three or four days after the birth, people inquire about
the child's name. According to the practice of that particular
family, the person whose prerogative it is to bestow the child's
name simply announces it.

Circumcision has never been part of the Dukku tradition in
this area. Among older men, none have been circumcised. However,
just within the past year or two, the idea has begun to circulate
among the younger men, and a few teen-age men — not many —
have been circumcised. Identical explanations have been given by
those who have been circumcised, and those who are thinking
about it: a sense of shame (in the accepted sense of the word).
They say that they can see no hygienic value in circumcision, nor
are they doing it for any religious motive. They are doing it so as
not to be laughed-at by men of other tribes[6] which practice circumcision! When some of these men see them — e. g., when they
are bathing — they are told that lack of circumcision is a sign of
backward people. Since only a very few Dukku men have had the
operation performed so far, it is still too early to determine
whether these few were individually influenced, or whether this is
a social influence at work which will eventually lead to the adop-
tion of the practice by the tribe as a whole.

---

[5] There are at least four young men now in their late twenties (it is hoped) who
were named Bature (European) because they happened to be born in the period from
July 1947 to October 1948 when the Editor was "touring" the Bakin Turu, Giro and
Ganwo areas. The arrival of the District Officer in a Dukku *Tunga* was a sufficient event
to warrant such a remembrance — or so they believed! *(Ed.)*

[6] To the Moslem, of course, circumcision is obligatory. It is almost certainly from
Moslems that the pressures will most likely come. See also Salamone *op. cit.* for some
parallel observations. One of the more ribald remarks frequently bandied about is to tell
an uncircumcised youth that he is so backward "he still has a tail". This is a pun on the
fact that the Hausa (or Hausa-ised) individual making the joke will know that in that
language *wutsiya* (tail) is a euphemism for penis — especially with children prior to circumcision. *(Ed.)*

It is interesting to note, however, that all of those Dukkawa who have already been circumcised are young men who travel fairly extensively — to different markets, *biki*, hunting and, therefore, have had much more contact with non-Dukkawa than the average Dukku man does. Formerly the Dukkawa, as with most other tribes, were a very closeknit society, but as the years have passed they have had more and more contact with peoples from other tribes. As this process of incorporation into the greater society outside of the tribe continues to develop, will the Dukkawa adopt the custom of circumcision or will they hold to their former practices?

## CHAPTER TEN

# LIFE-CYCLE: MARRIAGE

## A.  STAGES OF MARRIAGE.

The total process of Dukku marriage can be extended over a period of up to ten or eleven years, from the time the engagement takes place to the actual day when the woman goes to live in the man's house. Rather than give a detailed analysis of the various stages immediately, it will be better to begin with an over-all summary of the marriage process and then, once a basic pattern is established, go back and develop its different aspects.

The engagement is effected by the father of the boy. He will chose a girl for his son — and make the arrangements with the father of the girl. After agreement is reached, the first thing the boy himself will do is buy some tobacco — *mafarin taba*[1] — and give it to the girl's mother. From the time of engagement, the boy will be expected to visit the compound of the girl's parents once or twice a month to greet them.

As mentioned previously, the engagement immediately constitutes a joking-relationship between the suitor with the brothers and sisters of the girl, and between the girl and the brothers and sisters of her suitor. They become *abokan wasa* — friends of play — to each other.

At some time after the engagement, a time to be determined by the father of the girl, the dowry will be begun to be paid. This

---

[1] *Mafari* literally means "the beginning (of anything)". *Taba*, of course, means "tobacco".

is called *gormo*[2] and consists of work that the boy must do on his future father-in-law's farm. There is no exchange of money in the Dukkawa custom of dowry payment (which is noticeably different from the practices of other tribes in the area). After a boy has been making *gormo* for several years, he will begin to sleep with his future wife. The time when this may occur will again be determined by the girl's father. Finally, there is the *marriage biki* which is the official celebration, after which the girl will permanently move into her husband's house.

The above constitutes the general pattern of all Dukku marriages. Depending upon how old the boy is when the engagement is made, and how many years his future father-in-law expects him to make *gormo,* the entire process can take anything from five to ten or eleven years to work itself out.

1. *The engagement.* The ordinary way in which an engagement is arranged is for the father of the boy to see a girl whom he thinks will make a good wife for his son. The main characteristics which influence his judgement are the good reputation of the girl's family and the obedience and industry of the girl herself. When he finds such a girl, he will always first ask his son if he would be willing to marry the girl before he does anything else. The boy himself must agree to the choice, otherwise the father will not pursue the matter any further. It seems that there is no concern by a father to influence his son in agreement. In more than half the cases investigated, the men had refused girls whom their fathers had chosen. In this event, the matter is dropped. At a later date, the father may choose another and again approach his son about her, or the boy himself might choose a girl and mention it to his father. In either case, no formal engagement will be considered unless both the boy and his father agree.

Once the father and son agree, the boy's father will approach the father of the girl to inform him that his son would like to marry the girl. Privately, the girl's father and mother will discuss the possibility of an arrangement being arrived at. Paramount in

---

[2] As pointed out, this does not appear to be a Hausa word, although there is a word in the Zamfara dialect (an area in close proximity to the geographical location of the Dukkawa) *garme* which means "the area between two transverse ridges of hoeing", and thus can mean the amount of land actually hoed. *(Ed.)*

their consideration will be character of the boy's father — like father, like son[3] — as well as discussing the temperament and character of the boy. If it happens that the girl's parents are not well acquainted with the boy's family, they will defer their answer until they have had time to investigate through friends or relatives. Once the girl's parents agree among themselves, they will ask the girl herself if she has any choice in the matter. Her agreement is not as necessary as is that of the boy to his father's choice. Most of the women with whom the question was discussed said they agreed to marry their parent's choice. This is at the initial step of the engagement: cases are known, however, of Dukku girls who have broken engagements after several years . . . . possibly because they were too young at the time of the engagement to make a valid choice. When there is full agreement between the parents of the boy and the girl, however, and between the parties themselves, the father of the girl will then so inform the boy's father. This step thus constitutes the actual engagement.

The girl is usually younger than the boy when the engagement takes place, but not noticeably so. Among some tribes in Nigeria there can be an age-gap of ten years or more between the man and the woman. This is usually the case among tribes which demand a large monetary dowry with the result that the boy has to spend many years accumulating the sum. He will therefore often choose a very young girl, sometimes in primary school, so that she will not be too far into child-bearing age when the time comes for marriage. For example, if a man cannot raise the dowry until he is twenty-five or twenty-six years old, he does not want to marry a woman of the same age. He would prefer someone about sixteen or seventeen. This means that if he negotiates for a wife when he is in his mid-teens, he will choose a girl who is six or seven years old. But such is not the case with the Dukkawa, probably because there is no monetary dowry. The age difference between the boy and the girl is seldom more than three years.

The Dukkawa themselves say that the engagement to marry can take place when the children are as young as six or seven years old. This might be true — more so in the girl's case — but it would

---

[3] Which says quite a lot for the way these children are regarded and brought up.

appear that such an age must be regarded as the minimum age at which the agreement can properly be reached. Most of the cases examined in detail — plus others more casually investigated — indicate that the boy is usually ten to twelve years old, and the girl is about nine or ten years old when the engagement process begins. Of course, these are average ages arrived at from a study of only forty or fifty cases. It does not mean therefore that all boys and girls are engaged at these respective ages. A few girls are known who, at six years of age, are already engaged. On the other hand, boys of thirteen and fourteen — and girls of eleven and twelve — who are not engaged yet are also known, although unengaged girls at this age are more rare. In most cases when a boy is past twelve years old and not engaged, it means that he previously rejected his father's choice and it has been agreed that he himself will chose his own bride.

2. *Mafarin taba.* "The initial tobacco." Although this is a very small thing in itself, it is a very strict part of the marriage process — so much so that the people say that if its observance is neglected, a marriage will never take place. Not only *must* it be observed, but, as far as can be ascertained, the Dukku are the only tribe which have this precise requirement.

As soon as the father of the girl informs the boy's father of his agreement to the marriage of his daughter, the very first thing the boy will do is to go to market and purchase some tobacco. One penny's worth! Even the amount of tobacco that is bought seems to be specified, since all the Dukkawa talked to mentioned exactly "one penny's worth," no more, no less.

The tobacco capable of being purchased for one penny is a twist about the size of a man's large finger. The boy will return home with it and give it to one of his sisters, preferably an older sister if he has one, and she in turn will take it to the mother of the future wife. The tobacco must be bought by the boy to be given to the girl's mother. However, as noted earlier, as soon as the engagement is made, *kunya* exists between the boy and his future mother-in-law, and he will never more even address her by her proper name: Thus, he himself cannot take the tobacco and give it to her personally.

When the girl's mother receives the tobacco, she will break it apart into very small flakes and distribute them among all the relatives of the boy and the girl who are intending to be married. This is a mere formality, but a strict one, even though no one is going to smoke a piece so small. When the mother distributes the tobacco, she will inform the recipients of her purpose in doing so. Female relatives of the boy and the girl will give the piece of tobacco to their husbands or older brothers; men will simply put it in their tobacco pouches along with their other tobacco.

No Dukkawa questioned knew of any marriage which has ever taken place when this custom was not observed.

3. *Engagement greeting.* After the engagement has been decided upon by the fathers of the boy and the girl, the boy is expected to manifest his respect for the girl's father by occasionally going to his house to greet him. He will do this several times a month and will usually go at night time, or in the very late evening when his own daily work is done, and when it is the time of day when the girl's father is most likely to be at home.

However, for the first few years, the boy himself will not personally greet his future father-in-law. He will always go with another boy. When they reach the girl's compound, the boy himself will not enter the compound, but will stay outside while his friend enters to extend his greeting to the man and to his family. "So-and-so is outside and has asked me to greet you for him."

After a brief exchange concerning the welfare of both compounds, the boy's friend comes out and they then return home. The boy himself is not invited into the compound, nor does the 'father-in-law' or any one else from the compound come outside to speak with him. The boy might also have brought some gift for the man — e. g. tobacco or kola nuts — which his friend would offer when he enters the compound.

When the boy has been making *gormo* — working on his prospective father-in-law's farm for a couple of years, he will come for one of these evening greetings and the man will invite him into the compound. From that time on (he will not require a second invitation) the boy will be permitted to enter the compound on the occasion of these visits and will then personally greet the man and his family.

4. *Wasa* — play. This kind of play means familiarity or joking-relationship. There are two aspects of this *wasa* in the marriage process.

> I. a. between boy and his *fiancée's* brothers and sisters.
>  b. between girl and her *fiancé's* brothers and sisters.
>
> II. between boy and girl themselves.

As soon as the engagement is arranged, an immediate relationship is established between the boy and the girl's brothers and sisters, and between the girl and the boy's brothers and sisters. This is the relationship of special familiarity by which they become *abokan wasa* — friends of play.

In general, it gives them the right to joke with each other, playfully mock each other, and even play practical jokes on one another. Whenever there is a group of boys or girls, if two people share this relationship they will tend to stay together and do things together. They will hold hands as they walk (which, incidentally, is more a custom of men than of women in this part of Nigeria) or put an arm across each other's shoulder. As much as possible, they will arrange to do things together, e. g. bathing, going to market, etc.

Because of the distinction between men's life and women's life in this society, this relationship of *wasa* will not be so manifestly expressed between a boy and a girl, for instance, between the boy and a sister of his future wife. They certainly will not go places together or do things together. The familiarity between them will be expressed whenever they happen to meet by joking remarks or by mocking criticisms. A girl might tell a boy that she hears his father had to carry his hoe to the farm because it was too heavy for him; the boy, in his turn, might answer after that it was a shame that three dogs died in their compound after eating the left-over *tuwo* which the girl cooked, etc.

One thing is to be noted concerning this *wasa* relationship. A girl will never joke with an older brother of the boy she will marry, although the relationship exists between them, and he can freely joke with her. In this case, the special respect which is due to the senior son is extended to all the brothers of the boy who are his senior. As one Dukku man expressed it, "The senior brothers are like fathers to the girl," and nobody in this society jokes with their fathers! Even the boy, on his part, although he will joke with the girl's older brothers, will do so very circumspectly, showing them the same respect he shows to his own older brothers.

The other aspect of *wasa* — between the boy and girl themselves — is expressed in the same way by joking and playful mockery. But whereas the former type of *wasa* primarily serves a social function whereby the members of the two families become better acquainted, the *wasa* between the boy and the girl has a more practical purpose — to determine if the future spouses are, or can become (if they are not), temperamentally and psychologically compatible with each other. It is not a phenomenon characteristic of the Dukkawa alone that there are people who cannot take a joke — even when they know with certainty that only a joke was intended. On the other hand, every person has certain things about which he or she does not want to joke. It is far better for people to find these out when they are young and when the effects are inconsequential, rather than later in life when adjustment is more difficult and understanding is frequently challenged by suspicion.

There is no definite time when this state of *wasa* between a boy and a girl begins. It is not an automatic status arising from the engagement, as is the former type, but a practical means towards a desired goal. When the boy is permitted to enter the compound of his future father-in-law to greet him and his family, as described immediately above, the circumstances will be congenial enough after a few visits for a few moments of *wasa,* and its duration will increase as time goes on.

The place of this *wasa* is in the girl's hut, but the boy and girl are never inside the hut alone. She will be there with some of her sisters, and the boy will usually bring one or more of his junior brothers, as a brother senior to the boy will not enter the girl's hut for *wasa.* Parents and older people are never present. The decision as to compatability will eventually be made by the boy and the girl themselves.

At the time of *wasa* the boy always returns to his own compound at night. There will come a time, when the girl is fully mature and has expressed her approval of the boy, that her father will invite the boy to remain overnight in his compound. The time of *wasa* is then finished: the girl has given her approval and the mere fact that the boy continues to come is a sufficient indication of his own. The father's invitation to stay overnight is, in fact, the grant of his permission for the boy to begin sleeping with his daughter.

5. *Gormo.* This is the name given to the way in which the boy will pay dowry for his future bride, i. e. the reimbursement he will make to his future father-in-law for taking his daughter away. For a specified number of years — the father-in-law will determine how many — the boy will usually go to his farm four times a year, staying one full day each time he goes. On the respective days he will clear the land, plant, weed, and harvest. The crop will always be guinea-corn and the complete harvest from this farm will be given to the girl's father. By common agreement, the Dukkawa value this harvest at one pound (twenty shillings). Although *gormo* is a matter of work rather than of money, this monetary valuation is necessary in the case when a man has made all, or part, of his *gormo* for a girl, and then the girl refuses to marry him. Before another man can marry the girl, the former suitor must be repaid for the years of work he did, and this is done in money, and at the rate stated.

The number of years for making *gormo,* as well as the year that *gormo* will begin, is determined by the girl's father. Ordinarily it begins when the future father-in-law feels the boy is sufficiently developed physically to do a good day's work, — around ten or eleven years old — and the average number of years engaged in *gormo* is five or six. Cases are known of a couple of men who made *gormo* for eight and nine years, but this is an exceptionally long time.

If the boy is older when the engagement is arranged, he may well be asked to begin *gormo* the first year. If the boy is younger at the time of his engagement — e. g. seven or eight years old — no prearrangement is made as to the year that *gormo* will start. The girl's father will wait until he thinks the boy is capable of doing the work, and then send word to the boy's father. It occasionally happens that if the boy's father thinks he is still too young he may ask that the beginning of *gormo* be postponed a year. This will always be granted although the number of years that the boy has

to work at *gormo* will not be changed. It just means that the boy
will be one year older when he gets married.

Although the father-in-law indicates the area to be farmed, he
does not specify any precise boundaries, for the main purpose of
*gormo* is not to add to the guinea-corn supply but to impress the
girl's father that the boy is good worker and, therefore, will be a
steady and reliable provider for the girl he intends to marry. So it
is left to be seen how much land the boy can farm in one hard
day's work, and how well he farms it.

In effect, a considerable piece of land usually gets cultivated,
for two reasons. First of all, all the Dukku boys take this charge
very seriously, not just to impress their future father-in-law, but to
impress everyone else as well. It must be remembered that they
are at an age — around ten or eleven years — when they are involved
in the transition from being a boy to becoming a man. As yet,
they have not done full-time farming with the adult men from
their compound, and they are the more anxious to seize this opportunity — even for four days scattered through the farming
season — to prove that they are capable of holding-their-own in
the adult world. The second reason is that other boys who are also
making *gormo* will 'team up' to help another on the days he goes
to his future father-in-law's farm (and the boy will help them in
their turns).

The first impression would be that calling for assistance
would be a negative mark against the boy, in that he would not
be able to do the work well enough if he did it alone. On the
contrary, however, it is a definite positive factor in the eyes of the
girl's father, i. e. here is a boy who will always have friends to
whom he can turn if the need arises. As to whether the other boys
will work as hard as the future husband himself, it is certain the
boy would not have called them if there was any doubt in his
mind! He not only wants to show that he has friends, but, especially, that he has hard-working friends. Of course any one deliver-
ing less than one hundred per-cent would know what his own
chances would be of getting this particular boy to help him when
his time for *gormo* comes!

The urge to prove oneself is further portrayed by certain
customs which are attached to the making of *gormo*. The boy will

not eat or drink anything (even water) on the days that he is making *gormo*. He will not smoke or chew anything. He will not talk to anyone other than to greet them with a simple "Hello." However, on days when several boys work together, one might bring a drum — for the quick tempo of drumming inspires an equally quick tempo of working — and on these occasions the boys will sing as they work.

When there is singing, it will usually be the *wakar gormo* — "song of the *gormo*" — that is sung. There is a selection of about twenty songs for use by boys making *gormo*. When a new boy begins to make *gormo*, he chooses one of these tunes for his own, and his name will be inserted into the song. It is even possible that the boy, if he is sufficiently talented, will compose his own new song. This *gormo* song becomes part of his life. When, even years later, a boy dies, the women who come to dance at his funeral *biki* will sing this song, since it is associated with the time he was courting his girl.

If a Dukku man marries a second wife, he will still have to make *gormo* for her. But since he is usually older at this time, the *gormo* will be for a fewer number of years.

In the case when a married woman leaves her husband, if she is leaving for another man, the new man must pay the *gormo* to the husband. If, however, she is not leaving in favor of another man, but just because of her dislike for her husband, the husband gets nothing (since there is no one to repay it). If someone decides to marry her, though, the obligation is still binding and the new man will have first to pay before marrying the woman.

In the final year of *gormo*, when the harvesting is done, the future father-in-law will invite the young man and the friends who helped him to a small celebration. The man will provide guinea-corn beer and might even have some food prepared. It is a casual occasion the main significance of which is not its festivity but the acknowledgement that the stipulation of *gormo* has been satisfactorily accomplished.

6. *Sleeping together.* The time that a boy begins to sleep with his girl is determined by the girl's father. The boy has been coming for several years to greet his future in-laws, and has been making *wasa* with the girl for a long enough time to enable her to

judge whether or not they will be compatible spouses. So, on one of the evenings when the boy comes to visit, the girl's father will privately converse with his wife about the possibility of the boy beginning to sleep with their daughter. The father will have determined that the girl is sufficiently mature at this time to have intercourse, and the parents will discuss the boy's character and ambition. If they are in agreement that the time is opportune, the father will wait until the boy is preparing to return home that night and suggest to him that he stay in the compound.

As mentioned previously, this invitation is understood by all parties concerned as permission for the boy to begin sexual relations with the girl. Once the girl's father makes the initial invitation, the boy will need no further invitations on future occasions to stay in the compound overnight.

This invitation will only occur after the boy has been making *gormo* for several years, but it may do so two or three years before the Marriage *Biki* when the girl actually leaves her parent's compound for permanent cohabitation with her husband.

7. *Marriage Biki.* The formalities and ceremonies attendant on this event will be presented in chapter twelve, but a few aspects of it must be examined here in order to achieve a full understanding of the marriage cycle.

The Marriage *Biki* is the major event in the life of any Dukku man or woman. It is the time when the woman becomes officially and publicly recognized as the man's wife, since it is the time she makes her complete separation from her family and moves into her husband's compound to become a full-time wife. Even though they have been having conjugal relations for two or three years previously, and the woman has frequently borne a child by this time — or is pregnant — the Dukku status of "married" is not fully applied to her until she makes this final break with her family.

The termination of *gormo* is the prerogative of the girl's father, but the time and date of the Marriage *Biki* is completely in the hands of the husband. Once his obligations are fulfilled — *gormo* — every husband wants his wife to come to her new home as soon as possible. However, the Marriage *Biki* is an expensive affair — according to Dukku standards — costing the husband any amount from fifteen to thirty pounds (forty to eighty dollars) according to the elaboration of the preparations. And since this is the major event in the man's life, he will never settle on a date until he feels he can provide the best of everything — within his foreseeable means — for those whom he invites to share his happiness. This means that several years usually elapse between the time *gormo* ends and the Marriage *Biki* is held.

The above concludes the general description of the marriage process from the time the engagement is arranged between the respective fathers to the day when the woman actually moves into her husband's home. Before leaving the question, a few observations must be made as to how the Dukkawa themselves consider marriage as a whole, especially in reference to the binding nature of the association of the two people as the years progress.

"Do you have a wife?" and "Are you married?" would ordinarily be considered in most societies as two ways of asking the same question; in other words, the same response would be expected to either of them. This is *not* the case with the Dukkawa. In response to the question, "Do you have a wife?", any Dukku boy or girl — even if only eight or nine years old — will respond, "Yes", if their parents have settled on an engagement. On the other hand, a man who has one or two children will be asked how long he has been married, and he will answer that he is not married yet! For the Dukkawa, "having a wife" can mean nothing more than knowing the girl that one will eventually marry; whereas "being married" usually signifies that the Marriage *Biki* has taken place and the woman is living in the man's home. In this sense, having sexual relations does not pertain to 'marriage' as such.

On the other hand, once a man has begun sexual relations with the girl he intends to "marry," she is in a special way considered "his woman". This would seem to point simply to a difference in terminology, namely, that what is commonly considered marriage — when a man and woman consent to live with each other — really occurs at the time the two people consent to sleep together; whereas the Marriage *Biki* — which the Dukkawa say constitutes "being married" — is merely public solemnization of a bond that already exists.

This could very well be the case. Unfortunately, with all simple solutions there is usually a snag, and so it seems with this one. After the Marriage *Biki,* when a BaDukku has become "married", he can dismiss his wife providing he has grounds which are considered a sufficient reason for his doing so, according to Dukku custom. However, before the Marriage *Biki* a BaDukku can decide he does not want to "marry" the girl — or the girl can decide this — and the whole arrangement can be then called off for no reason at all. It would seem therefore that the marriage is somehow regarded as being more firmly established at the time of the Marriage *Biki.*

When a woman delivers a child before the Marriage *Biki,* the child remains in her parent's compound and is considered to belong to that family until the Marriage *Biki* when the woman moves into her husband's compound.

The Dukkawa themselves are not accustomed to the precision of modern society. They are not able to specify the exact time that a marriage bond takes effect. Some simply answer that they do not know, or that they are just following the customs handed down to them by their forefathers. Among those who attempt to specify the moment of marriage, there are varying opinions. Some say it is the night after the Marriage *Biki* ends and the woman enters her husband's hut for the first time. Others say it is when the couple begin sleeping together. A few even mention the time of engagement, when the boy and girl are little more than children, as constituting the bond — although they readily admit the tenuous nature of the relationship at this early stage.

The situation has been presented here as the Dukkawa themselves consider it. No observer can offer a deeper understanding of Dukku marriage than the Dukkawa themselves express.

B.   SEXUAL AND MARITAL ETHICS.

The celibate state is unknown to the Dukkawa. Marriage is an integral part of their lives, as witnessed by the fact that engagements are arranged at so early an age and that the pre-marriage formalities are a continuous process for a period of up to ten years. To find any BaDukku who did not subscribe to this pattern of life would be as likely as finding a BaDukku who did not know how to farm.

As has been stressed from the beginning, the two main groups of Dukkawa involved in this survey are those who trace their area of origin to the town of Dukku and those who look to Iri as being their original area. A BaDukku from Dukku will always marry a Dukku-Dukku woman, and a BaDukku from Iri will always marry an Iri-Dukku woman. Only in the case when there are no available women from the specific branches of the tribe (they say) would they consider marrying a woman from another branch, i. e. a Dukku-BaDukku marrying an Iri-Dukku woman. No cases were found of any existing marriages of this kind.

The Dukkawa do admit the possibility of intermarrying with other tribes "if both sides agree", but then simply add that "both sides *never* agree!" No cases are known, nor have any ever been heard of, Dukku marrying anyone other than Dukku.

By custom, the Dukkawa are neither monogamous nor polygamous, i. e. as a tribe they have no particular tendency towards having only one wife. The Dukkawa in the surveyed area are about evenly divided between those who have one wife and those who have two wives. If there is a difference, the one-wife Dukkawa, though it may be a mere matter of opinion, would predominate. Only one Dukku man has been encountered who has three wives. This is noteworthy in view of the fact that the general area in which the Dukkawa live is almost completely a Moslem and pagan environment, and Islamic law permits the taking of four lawful wives. Among the various indigenous pagan tribes in the area, the Dukkawa undoubtedly tend the most strongly towards monogamy.

The Dukkawa have their own ideas as to degrees of consanguinity and affinity, but they are unanimous in their agreement that no Dukkawa can marry a *relative*. This no-relative marriage extends at least to include first cross-cousins, as shown by the following example. For simplification, Christian names will be employed, but the case did actually occur.

John wanted to marry Mary, but he could not because both were related to Joseph. John was Joseph's nephew "by blood" and Mary was Joseph's niece "by marriage." Public opinion would not permit the marriage to take place.

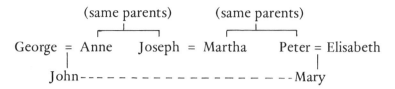

The custom of *levirite marriage* is practiced, i. e. a man marrying his deceased brother's wife, but not on a basis of absolute necessity. For instance, it is not mandatory that a woman remarry when her husband dies, although almost all young and middle-aged women do. In the case of a woman who did not remarry, or at least not immediately, she would return to her parent's compound.

In most cases a levirite marriage will be proposed between the woman and a *junior* brother of the deceased husband. She will never marry a senior brother of the man owing to his special position in the family (as one BaDukku succinctly explained it, "the senior brother is like a father to the woman").

Although this levirite marriage is the general custom, both the man and the woman are free to refuse though in cases when this refusal occurs, it is most often on the part of the man.

There is a particular example which illustrates some of these points (again this is an actual case).

> Charles was nineteen years old and has completed his years of *gormo* — dowry payment — but he had not yet had his Marriage *Biki.* So his intended wife was still living in her parent's compound.
> Then Charles died from a snakebite and a marriage was arranged between Mary and Matthew, Charles' fifteen year old younger brother. Within four months after Charles' death, Matthew and Mary were married and Mary left her parent's compound.

It was understood why the marriage was arranged between the girl and Charles' younger brother, but enquiry was made as to why the marriage was not postponed a couple of years since fifteen years of age was young even by Dukku standards.

The boy's father replied that in the ordinary course of events, the marriage would have been delayed, but special circumstances dictated that the marriage take place as soon as possible.

First of all, since the *gormo* — dowry — had been paid, Mary strictly belonged to the deceased Charles. Then the arrangement was transferred to a marriage between Matthew and Mary, both parties agreeing. But since there had been no Marriage *Biki* as yet, Mary could not enter Matthew's compound!

Secondly, as long as the Marriage *Biki* was postponed, Mary had to live apart from Matthew in her parent's compound and there was the possibility that other men would begin to court her. Since Mary was already pregnant (by Charles), a prompt marriage between Mary and Matthew permitted them to begin living together and assured her of a place in the family.

A husband can dismiss his wife if she manifests "bad character", such as refusing to do her work properly, selling her husband's goods, constant bickering with neighbors which necessarily diminishes the husband's reputation, etc. In the case of such a dismissal, nothing is given to the woman except her own personal belongings. Although this happens, it is a rare occurrence indeed since the woman highly values her security within the family structure. Not only would shame be attached to any such dismissal, but the known fact would constitute a serious obstacle to the possibility of the woman's remarriage.

A wife is free to leave her husband but this is also a rarity for the reasons just mentioned. If such a case occurs, any man wishing to marry the woman will first have to pay the monetary value of the *gormo* — dowry payment — which the husband performed to obtain his wife, i. e. one pound for every year the husband worked on his father-in-law's farm.

*Intercourse.* A woman will continue sexual relations with her husband until the sixth or seventh month of pregnancy. Intercourse will be resumed three or four months after delivery. This is in stark contrast to the customs of many other tribes in Nigeria where the women will not have sexual relations from nine months to three years after bearing a child. It is believed in these circumstances that intercourse affects lactation and that the child will not be weaned properly. A Dukku husband will not have relations with his wife during her menstrual periods nor will he or any other person eat food which the woman has prepared during these days of the month.

*Fornication and adultery.* Although these situations occur, as a group the Dukkawa would have to be classed as being very moral on this issue. One obvious reason is the manner of life in which they live, i. e. until recently they have had very little contact with peoples outside their own group. Within this secluded environment, where everyone knows what everyone else is doing, a man's (or woman's) good reputation is a thing to be most highly prized if any minimum of happiness and security is to be expected.

Added to this, there has been a long tradition — within the Dukku tribe itself — of strict observance of morality in this regard. Fights have been observed that have taken place between Dukku men for the mere reason that one man talked to the betrothed of another. Even if it was only intended to be in joke, there are some things the Dukkawa do not joke about!

*Contraception.* The role of children in Dukku society pertains to the integrity of their domestic structure. As one man told me, the most important thing in his life was to have as many children as possible to carry on his name after he dies. And this is not merely one man's opinion, it is the typical attitude of Dukkawa as regards their ultimate goal in this life. In view of this fact, it is not difficult to understand that contraception is seldom practiced. It is never practiced simply for the sake of not having children. The only instance when the Dukkawa themselves admit to the practice of contraception is in the case of a woman who has had extreme difficulty in giving birth to her last child and it is generally accepted that another child would cost her her life. Even in such cases some women will refuse any contraceptive treatment. They feel strongly that their one, and only, purpose in life is to provide children for their husband.

When contraception is employed, the medicine is made from the pounded roots of a certain kind of a tree.[4] These roots are cooked and mixed with guinea-corn gruel — *kunu* — which is drunk by the woman. Since this type of medicine is not frequently

---

[4] One widely recognised contraceptive and abortifacient is *shuni*, small cones of prepared indigo *(baba)*, Indigofera Arrecta, I. Tinctoria or I. Anil. It is also employed as a purgative and specific in stomach ailments in horses and donkeys. *(Ed.)*

used, most of the Dukkawa are unfamiliar with its preparation and a special person will have to be called on to make it.

*Abortion.* For the reasons just mentioned concerning the Dukku attitude towards children, abortion is not a widespread practice either. The obvious case is when an unmarried girl conceives by someone other than her future husband, and even here the Dukkawa themselves have divided opinions. Some, while certainly not condoning the action, will still never consider permitting an abortion, saying, "Somehow God wanted this child to be." Other Dukkawa will feel an abortion is permissable.

If an abortion is decided upon, within the first three months of pregnancy, the girl's mother will prepare the medicine from the leaves of the *tsada* tree — wild plum.[5] These will be cooked with guinea-corn gruel — *kunu* — and drunk by the girl.

One older Dukku man has stated there was another circumstance in which an abortion would be performed. He said it has been known that some fathers have ordered their daughters to abort, even though the girl conceived by her future husband. The circumstance is that the boy is still making *gormo* — dowry payment — and the girl's father fears the boy will stop once he knows the girl is pregnant. As long as the "husband" and "wife" agree for each other, how could the girl's father prohibit the marriage once the girl has borne a child? Although this is a plausible circumstance, it is doubtful if it occurs very often. First of all, there is the Dukkawa's high regard for the rearing of children. Secondly, the added amount of guinea-corn which the girl's father will receive from two or three more years of *gormo* — the boy only works four days a year — does not seem to be a sufficient reason to perform abortion. Thirdly, the specified number of years which the boy is supposed to make *gormo* before he can take his wife is generally known to both families. There is no possibility that the boy could convince people that he has completed the specified obligation. Fourthly, from the time the boy begins sleeping with his intended bride, they have full sexual rights with each other. The only thing remaining is the Marriage *Biki* when the girl comes to live in her

---

[5] Ximenia Americana. A small tree with yellow plum-like fruits, rather acid in taste which make an excellent jelly fully comparable to quince. *(Ed.)*

husband's house. The case described would have to occur when the boy was fifteen or sixteen years old, or when intercourse had been undertaken surreptitiously, and it would be unlikely at that age that he would possess the financial means to arrange the kind of Marriage *Biki* that would be expected of him.

## CHAPTER ELEVEN

# LIFE-CYCLE: DEATH

## A.   IN GENERAL

"What will happen to you when you die?" In answer to this question, the Dukkawa express various vague generalities which bespeak of some kind of belief in an after-life. Some say a good man's spirit will be at rest — although nothing specific about the kind of rest — but a bad man's spirit will be imprisoned in the ground to suffer — again, nothing specific about the kind of suffering. There does not seem to be any developed cult about being rejoined with or separated from ancestors.

But the most accurate answer to the above question which typifies the general attitude of the Dukkawa concerning death was given by a very simple and honest BaDukku: "How do I know what will happen to me when I die? I have never died before!" Simple people almost always hit on the basic premise of philosophical truth, namely that knowledge comes from some sort of previous experience. To a person from the "educated" world where there are answers for everything — sometimes partial answers which are blown up into a semblance of absolute truths — it is edifying to find a people who do not know an answer . . . and who will readily admit the fact!

## B.   WHEN A PERSON DIES.

It is best to give a general description of conventional behaviour when a person dies, after which the particular points which need clarification and which accentuate Dukku customs in this matter can be re-examined.

137

When a person dies, there are two occasions when the people gather to pay their respects. The first time is on the day on which or the day after, the death occurs which is when the Burial Service takes place. As many people as can be notified, and have the opportunity to come on this short notice, will attend. The second occasion will be at a later date — from a month to several years — when a proper Funeral *Biki* can be prepared for the deceased, It's date will be announced two or three weeks before the event takes place, and all the Dukkawa from the immediate area — as well as many from as far as ten or more miles away — will come to attend.

As pointed out in the section on Birth, there is no special Burial Service for the death of a newborn child. Naturally, therefore, there is no Funeral *Biki* either.

For an unmarried teen-age boy or girl, there will be both a Burial Service and a Funeral *Biki,* but on a smaller scale than for a married person. It is only after a person is married that he, or she, is considered to have entered the complete state of life, and it is to these that the full Burial Service and Funeral *Biki* is accorded.

## C.   DAY OF DEATH AND BURIAL SERVICE.

When a death occurs, the body is immediately taken into the personal hut, where it will be prepared for the burial. If the death occured in the morning, the burial will be in the late afternoon or evening, before dark. If someone dies in the evening or at night, the burial service will be the following morning about ten o'clock.

After the body is removed to the hut for preparation, it will be washed and the head will be shaved. Then it will be covered with a cloth and will remain in the hut until the time for it to be carried to the grave.

As soon as a person dies, drumming will commence to announce the fact. If there is no drum in the compound, someone will be sent to the nearest drummer, who will immediately begin the drumming from his own compound. There are various types of drums which the Dukkawa use and they will be fully described in the Chapter on *Biki*. The drum used for the purpose of making known a death is the largest of these drums, called a *ganga.* It is held in front of the body by a leather strap across the shoulder. The drumming is done by using a curved stick with the right hand and by concordant beating with the left hand. Although the Dukkawa do not have a highly developed style of drumming, such as the "talking drums" of the Yoruba, there is a special "death beat" which all people will recognize. There is a particular "death beat" for a man and a different beat for a woman, although no more specific knowledge as to the person who died can be conveyed by the drumming.[1]

As soon as the people hear the drumming indicating that a man or a woman has died, they will wait to be informed of the person's identity. This information will not be long in coming. Dispatching messengers is the first thing the master of the compound, or the one in authority at the time, will see to. These messengers, usually older boys, will go to all the compounds in the immediate area. People from these compounds, in turn, will carry the news further, and so on.

The news will be transmitted as far away as the person who died was known. Within two hours after death, everyone will know that a man or woman has died (drumming) and exactly who that person was (messengers).

A good example is the case of an older man who recently died. His death occured at eight-thirty in the morning. Seven hours later when the burial took place, at three-thirty in the afternoon, one hundred and fifty Dukku men and women had gathered at his compound for the service. The furthest distance traveled to the burial was eight miles! Considering the amount of time it takes to "walk" a message to a distance of eight miles, as well as the eight miles, the person must walk back to the place after he has received the message — sixteen miles in seven hours — the speed of this "bush telegraph" is only overshadowed by the promptitude with which the Dukkawa respond to such information.

The site for the grave is chosen by the master of the house — or the eldest son in the case of the master's death. It is always *outside* the compound (there are some tribes which occasionally bury their dead within the compound) but not usually more than

[1] The same, indeed, could be said of the "Death Knell" as still rung in English Churches. Nine strokes for a man, eight for a woman. The function is identical. *(Ed.)*

fifty yards distant. On occasion, a person will not be buried at the compound where he, or she, died. Although it is not an absolute, a first son might be buried near his paternal grandfather and this might be several miles away. Also, a widow who has not remarried and returned to her former compound most likely will be buried near her husband when she dies.

In each area, there is a special group of nine or ten elders who are designated as the official grave-diggers for *all* burials except those of very young children. As soon as they receive information concerning the person who died, they assemble at that person's compound. When sufficient time has been allotted for them to arrive, the ones who have come will begin the grave, working one at a time. One man will work for ten minutes, then the next man, and so on. For this work they receive payment in money, guinea-corn, fowl, etc. In the case just referred to above, nine grave-diggers alternated the work and received a total of two pounds and ten shillings — roughly eight shillings apiece — as well as small amounts of foodstuffs. The relatives of the deceased will always make some payment to these men, but they also receive donations from other people. The reason is that these elders are held in special esteem and any donation to them is an outward recognition of their status.

The grave itself is usually not more than three feet deep. The width is from two and a half to three feet, and the length is deter-mined by measuring the body of the deceased. A long cornstalk is laid next to the body and broken about six inches beyond the body measurement. Then the cornstalk is taken to the site which has been chosen for the grave, laid on the ground, and the length of the grave is marked off. It does not seem that there is any specified direction in which the length of the grave must be aligned. Most of the graves observed were laid out in a general east — west alignment, but there are a sufficient number north — south graves to question whether there is any strict policy in this matter.[2]

---

[2] It is recorded that tribes in some areas sometimes exhume a corpse for reburial at another location. I have never heard of this being practiced by any of the tribes in the Yelwa area. It is certainly not the practice of the Dukkawa. However, Dukkawa have been known to unearth a grave in order to bury a second person in the same place. — This will *never* be done unless several years have elapsed since the first burial. This is

While the elders are working on the grave, men and women are steadily arriving for the burial service. Very few people will actually enter the compound. The men will gather together in their groups, and the women in theirs. Grass mats will be bought for the more important men — i. e. older men — to sit on. Everyone will be offered water to drink after their journey but, because of the nature of the occasion, there has been very little time for preparations. The women of the compound will try to prepare some kind of food on this short notice, especially for those who might come from the farthest distances. Those from near-by compounds will generally refuse to eat even if they are offered food, out of consideration for the women who would otherwise have to prepare food for the considerable number of people involved.

The women will usually cook *kunu* — gruel — which is just guinea-corn flour and hot water, and which can be prepared quickly and in quantity.

As soon as thirty or forty people have arrived, a drummer will start to play the death beat. This will continue until everyone appears and the time comes for the body to be taken from inside the hut to the burial site.

Sometime before the actual burial, the members of the deceased man's family will have all their hair shaved from heads. If it is the master of the house who died, everyone — men and women — will have their heads shaved. If a husband dies, the wife's head will be shaved; if a wife dies, the husband will have *his* head shaved. If an older boy or girl dies, even a married one, the father ordinarily does not have his head shaved. The mother may or may not have her head shaved. But all the brothers and sisters will shave their heads.

If a husband dies, the wife will stay in her hut for the entire time the people who have come are gathered at the compound. A husband will do the same if his wife has died.

All the while there is the constant drumming. Although there are no specified dances that have to be performed at this burial service, various people usually do get up to dance.

---

not a frequent occurrence, but such an instance happened at the death of a middle-aged woman. Her husband had her buried together with his father (who had been dead for ten years). Among Moslems exhumation and reburial is absolutely forbidden.

At the Funeral *Biki*, which will be conducted at a later date and after due preparation, there will be specific groups who will dance as a special manifestation of respect for the person who died. At this burial service immediately after the death occurs, the elders who have come will usually do a short dance if the person who died was an elder.

If the deceased had been a hunter, which most Dukku men are, a group of hunters will stand up to do a dance. This particular dance starts outside the compound, led by one hunter who is carrying a loaded dane gun. The slow-shuffle dance, with the men chanting a hunting song, proceeds towards the hut in which the dead man's body lies. At the doorway of the hut, the procession stops and the lead hunter raises the gun and shoots it in the air. The symbolism is that the sound of a gun will never again be heard coming from the man of that hut.

If the person had been a blacksmith, any blacksmiths present might do a dance. Men who have their farms adjacent to that of the deceased might also do a dance. If a woman dies, her special friends might do a dance. In other words, people who shared any particular aspect of Dukku life with the person who died might appropriately gather together to perform a dance for the person.

There is a special custom of *wailing* which the teen-age girls observe. This is not performed for everyone who dies. It is not done for a young child, nor is it done for an older person. In the latter case, it is felt that the person had led a full life and the time for him (her) to die had come.

Wailing signifies that the person who died was called away from this life unexpectedly before he lived the full life he had hoped for.

When the girls do this wailing, they lean against the side of this person's hut, resting their heads on their forearms, and cry out. The ululation lasts about ten or fifteen seconds and may be done several times before the burial takes place. Although this custom is a sincere expression of sorrow, it is basically a ritual observance.[3]

---

[3] One of the first times I attended a burial, I arrived at the moment this wailing was taking place and really thought the girls had gone beserk. After a few seconds, one of the girls stopped crying, wiped her eyes, and greeted me with a smiling face. . . as if it had never occured. I was relieved to see she was in control of herself.

As the time for the burial approaches, a group of men will stand around the grave holding large pieces of cloth. These will be opened and held shoulder-high, hanging to the ground, screening the grave from the peoples' view. The purpose of this action is to hide the corpse and the grave at the time of burial.

At first it was suspected that this was some custom of respect in that it would be improper to witness a human body being put into the ground, or maybe that it had something to do with a final show of privacy to the deceased. These were logical suppositions based on symbolic inferences.

However, it was later discovered that this custom of screening the grave site with cloth is not a symbolic action at all, but that it is said to have application as a precaution. If people do not see the corpse or the grave, they cannot start rumors concerning the manner of death the person suffered, or even that something of value was put into the grave before it was filled in. Such an answer did not seem entirely satisfactory and it was suspected that there must be more to it than that, but the explanation was accepted since no other was forthcoming. It has since been learned — emphatically — that precaution against rumors is definitely *the* reason for screening the grave site!

The following actual incident did not occur among the Dukkawa, but among people of a neighboring tribe. However, it was "close enough to home" to banish any doubt that such things would be possible among the Dukkawa as well. A father and his son, and several other men, were traveling through the area. One morning the son woke up and did not feel well, and within two hours was dead. Since the men were twenty miles from their home, they decided to bury the boy at the place where he died. They simply dug a grave, interred the body, and covered it up. Later in the day a woman from the area (although she had not been present at the burial!) started the rumor that the men had hidden one hundred pounds (over two hundred and fifty dollars) in the grave with the boy's body.

There was very serious concern among the boy's relatives that someone would exhume the corpse in search of this non-existent money. For people all over the world, the term "final resting place" is an appropriate metaphor. For the Dukkawa it is more than a metaphor, it is a concept which is taken very seriously in almost the strictest sense of the word. Thus, the screening of the grave site at the time of burial is an added assurance that the person interred will rest in peace.

As one group of men gather around the grave site to screen it from the people's view, another group of five or six go to the hut to remove the body and carry it to the grave. The body, which is completely wrapped in a large coloth, is placed on a grass mat- *tabarma*- and taken outside the hut where a procession immediately forms behind those who are carrying it. The drumming continues during this procession but there is no singing or chanting. When the men bringing the body arrive at the grave site, the other men holding the pieces of cloth immediately encircle them. The only people within the "cloth screen" will be the five or six men who brought the body. These men are the ones who have been designated to perform the burial.

The body is set down next to the grave and the shroudcloth in which the body has been wrapped, is opened at the head just enough for it to be exposed. The grass mat on which the body has been carried is cut with a knife along the contour of the body. Then the body, resting on the remainder of the grass mat, is lowered by the men into the grave. The body is adjusted so that it is lying on its side in an apparent sleeping posture. No one says anything at this time. The grave is then immediately covered. This is mentioned because it is the custom of some tribes in this area, after the body is situated in the grave but before it is covered, for someone to "talk" to the corpse telling him they are sorry he has left them, that he will not be forgotten, etc.

As is the custom with several other tribes in this area, earth is never allowed to fall directly on the corpse. Sticks and branches are first placed on top of the grave. The sides of the grave have been dug at a slight angle — wider at the top and narrowing towards the bottom. The sticks that are placed above the corpse are measured so that they "fit in" the grave about two or three inches from the ground level, but still not touching the body. When all the sticks are in place, a grass mat is placed on top of them, and then the entire mat is "cemented" in position by packing mud on top of it. Finally a mound is built up using the earth that was removed when digging the grave. As this is being done, the men standing around the grave site will take down the "cloth screen."

As a final gesture, several calabashes will be broken on rocks and the pieces will be put on top of the dirt mound. Food is eaten from calabashes, water is drunk from calabashes, beer and guinea-corn gruel is drunk from calabashes, seeds are planted from calabashes, items are carried in calabashes, etc. The breaking of calabashes after someone's death is a sign that this most common utensil in Dukku life will no longer be needed by the person who has died.

When the burial is finished there are no further ceremonies and the visitors disperse.

## D. PERIOD OF MOURNING.

Whenever a married man or woman dies, there is a special period of mourning for the widow or widower. This lasts from the day the spouse dies until the time the Funeral Biki is held. This period can be from one month to a year. The following are the customs observed by a man or a woman under these circumstances.

1. For a Widow.

   1. She will keep her head shaved for the entire period of mourning. (If other relatives shave their heads at the time of the death, it will just be done that one time, then the hair will be allowed to grow.) Frequently she will also rub her head with a red dye made from cam-wood.[4]

   2. She will always wear a skirt made from leaves instead of wearing the piece of cloth that is ordinarily wrapped around the waist as a skirt. This "leaf skirt" is simply leaves that are put around the waist and kept in place with a piece of rope or thin cloth that is tied like a belt.

---

[4] Baphia Pubescens *(majigi)*. *(Ed.)*

3. A special cord made from Indian hemp is always worn around the waist. This is simply referred to as *igiya,* the Hausa word for "string", and is probably the main symbol of this mourning period. (There is a special ceremony attached to the removal of this *igiya* at the Funeral *Biki.*)

II. For a Widower.

1. He too will be required to wear this Indian hemp cord — *igiya* — from the day of his wife's death until the Funeral *Biki.*

2. He will always wear his loincloth inside-out.

3. He will never wear his cap.

E.   FUNERAL BIKI.

This final tribute to a person who died will be held as soon as possible after the death occurred, and at a time when people will have the opportunity to attend *i. e.* not when some men are absent on hunting trips, when the farming season is at its peak, etc. Since at least two hundred people can confidently be expected to attend (and possibly more) and since many will stay for three nights, it is not an occasion that can be prepared for quickly, or undertaken lightly.

Funeral *Biki* last for three days: people arrive in the late afternoon of the first day, stay through the second and third days, and depart on the morning of the fourth day. There will have to be food and sufficient guinea-corn beer.

The two considerations for the choosing of a time for the Funeral *Biki, i. e.* time to procure sufficient provisions and the selection of an opportune moment — usually result in several months elapsing between the actual death and the *Biki.* There are two seasons in the year when Funeral *Biki* are most likely to be held. The first is at the end of the Hot Season, around May, when most or all of the hunters are back from their trips but the farming season has not yet begun. The other time is in late December or January when the harvesting of the crops is finished and the hunters will not leave until late February or March.

Of the various types of *biki* — which will be summarized in the following chapter — the Funeral *Biki* is the only one which is incumbent. Most married couples have a marriage *Biki,* but there can be mitigating circumstances which permit it to be ommited. There can never be mitigating circumstances for the omission of Funeral *Biki*: it *must* be held.

If a man has died, preparations will be undertaken by his brothers and his senior son. If the senior son has reached maturity, he will have the main responsibility. If he is too young to assume this task, the eldest brother of the deceased will be in charge. If a woman has died, her husband will organize the Funeral *Biki*. For an elderly widow the responsibility falls on her eldest son.

As the day of the *biki* approaches, the grave will be decorated since, at the time of burial, it was just covered over with earth. The entire mound will be "plastered" with mud and hand polished to a smooth cement-like finish. Some object, like a pot or the horns of a small animal, might be plastered onto the top of the mound. The ground for ten or fifteen feet all around the grave site will be completely cleared of grass, rocks, or any small tree stumps, etc. so that the grave will be the immediate focus of attention for those who come to the ceremony.

The same relatives of the deceased who shaved their heads at the time of death will again shave their heads for the Funeral *Biki*, except that a widower, or a widow (whose head will have been shaved regularly throughout the mourning period), will not be shaved at this time.

On the first day of the Funeral *Biki* as the people gradually begin to arrive, there will be occasional drumming to announce the beginning of the affair. There is a different beat depending on whether a man or woman died. At first this drumming will only be done for a few minutes, with ten or fifteen minute intervals. The duration of drumming will then become longer, and the intervals shorter as more and more people continue to appear. By the time the sun goes down (the people begin arriving about five o'clock in the afternoon) the drumming will have become continuous. It should be noted here that not all the guests arrive on the evening of this first day. Those who do are usually the people who are coming from farther distances. Since the second day of the Funeral *Biki* – which is really the first full day – is considered the major event of the three-day occasion, those who live closer can wait and arrive early on the morning of the second day and still not miss any of the main ceremonies.

As a sign of mourning, the spouse of the deceased person will also remain in his or her hut on the first day of the Funeral *Biki*. Early on the morning of the second day, he (she) will go and stay inside the guest hut either alone or with a few friends. If there are some friends in attendance, none will either greet or talk to the relict. He or she will stay here in the guest hut until it is time for a group of women to come and lead him (her) outside for the ceremony which terminates the official mourning period.

The dancing that occurs at a Funeral *Biki* can generally be classified under two heads. First are the specific ceremonial dances done by certain definite groups in deference to the deceased. The last of these particular dances is that undertaken by the group of women who will lead the widower (widow) to the place where the mourning period is ceremoniously terminated.

When this ceremony is concluded, there will be drumming and general dancing by all the people for the remainder of the time of the Funeral *Biki*.

In outline, it can be analysed as follows:

    a. Particular ceremonial dances
    b. Termination of the mourning period
    c. General dancing

These special dances will be performed on the morning of the second day – i. e. first full day – of the Funeral *Biki*. They lead up to the ceremony which will conclude the period of mourning for the deceased person, a ceremony which usually takes place in the early afternoon. The general dancing thereafter goes on for the remainder of the second day and continues through the entire third day until late at night. When not dancing, the people are either drinking guinea-corn beer, smoking, talking, eating (not much) or sleeping.

The special dances preceding the ceremony which terminates

the mourning period can be done by almost any group of men (or women) who share a "common cause." Their dance will be representative of all people who participate in that cause.

For instance, a group of women who make pots might gather together to do a dance, or women who specialize in making guinea-corn beer, or men who are blacksmiths or leatherworkers, etc. These are just examples underlining the fact that almost any justification is sufficient for a group of people to join in a dance as long as all of them are somehow involved in one particular concern. These dances are optional and depend entirely on the whim of the participants at the time.

There are, however, some special dances which *must* be performed. Some of these must be done at all Funeral *Bikis*, others are performed only on certain occasions, usually determined by the particular occupation or by the achievements of the person who died.

One dance that is always done is performed by contemporaries and close friends of the deceased. Men will do this dance if a man has died; women will do the dance if a woman had died. It usually includes fifteen or twenty people of the same age group as the deceased, drawn from people who had grown up with him (her), sharing the same experiences of life at the same time. Those participating in this dance can all be young adults, or middle-aged, or elderly, depending upon the age of the dead person.

In the case of a man who died, the lead dancer will carry a special symbol of wrestling which conveys the message, "We wrestled together with this man as we were growing up together." Formerly, even as recently as about fifteen years ago, wrestling was as very organized sport between groups, and even areas, of the Dukkawa. Today it has lost much of its special significance and the prestige of previous years and is only performed rarely at social gatherings. Other than that, it is mostly a form of entertainment and a pastime when a group of boys or young men get together. According to Dukku custom in former times, and even today, a married man will not wrestle.

The wrestling symbol carried at *Biki* of this nature is a piece of wood, about two and a half to three feet in height, which is formed in the shape of a 'Y'. Sometimes it is merely cleaned and polished with oil, at other times there will be designs painted on it. As the people in the dance follow the leader who is carrying this 'Y' symbol, they do a slow shuffle dance around the compound and end at the doorway of the dead man's hut. While they are making this dance-procession, they are singing one of the traditional wrestling songs.

If it is a woman who has died, there will by this same kind of dance, but there is no particular symbolic object which is carried. There are various tunes which women sing or hum while they are grinding guinea-corn, and the women in this dance-procession will sing a particular one that was a favorite of the deceased woman.

The elders (men) will always do a dance for a deceased adult. In every area of four or five square miles, there are always half a dozen or so of these elderly men who hold a special position of honor and respect. At *biki* they sit together in the same place, food is brought to them first, and so on.

Whenever there is divided opinion concerning the traditions of the tribe, one or several of these elders will be consulted. It is in this aspect of epitomizing the traditions of the Dukku tribe that their dance at a Funeral *Biki* has its real significance. The elders dancing for the deceased person is a confirmation of the fact that he or she lived a good life according to Dukku standards.

The dance itself is a slow four or five step shuffling forwards and backwards — towards and away from the drummer who is standing in front of them — with a slight simultaneous swinging of the body from right to left. Since most of those participating will be over sixty years old, the dance cannot be too energetic! But it is edifying to see some of these very old men, who sometimes have difficulty in walking and who very seldom leave their compounds, nevertheless making the effort to stand up and dance at a Funeral *Biki*, if only for a few seconds. Just the fact that they came at all is a tribute in itself.

As mentioned in an earlier chapter when discussing *gormo* — the dowry payment which is done by farm work for the future father-in-law — young men making *gormo* tend to stick together and help each other. If it happens that a young man dies during the years he was making *gormo* the other young men in the area who are making gormo will perform a special rite for him at the Funeral *Biki.*

Six of these young men will gather outside the compound, usually in front of the guest hut and, to the beating of a drum, they will begin to dig up the ground. This symbolizes the farming the deceased young man was doing for *gormo*.

Each young man has his own hoe and they dig, one by one, for only a few seconds each. When all six of these men have performed their part, some guinea-corn beer is brought and one of the men pours the beer into the hole that has been dug. Then the soil is pulled back with the hoes and the hole is filled in.

The Dukkawa themselves give no reason for the pouring of beer into the overturned earth, except to say that "it has always been our custom." From close observation of their customs concerning *gormo,* it is thought that the guinea-corn beer might have originally had reference to the completion of the *gormo* obligation, i. e. when the final year of the farm work is done and the man is entitled to have his Marriage *Biki* and take his wife into his own compound.

When this final year of *gormo* is completed, the future father-in-law will buy several pots of guinea-corn beer for the young man and his friends as a sign that he is satisfied that the *gormo* requirement has been fulfilled. The guinea-corn beer which is poured into the spot that has been turned over at a Funeral *Biki* for a young man who never completed his *gormo* could possibly have been intended originally as a symbolic termination of the *gormo* obligation or as an abrogation of that obligation.

As pointed out earlier, to a greater or lesser degree, all Dukku men can be classified as "hunters". It would certainly be an oddity to find an adult Dukku man who had never been on a hunting trip. This being the case, a group of the better hunters, those men who have killed "Big Animals", such as roan antelope, hartebeest, (sometimes warthog) will always do a dance in honor of a deceased man. While they are performing it, they will sing one of the particular songs which is sung by the hunters returning from a successful hunt.

When all of these special dances have been completed, several women wearing only leaves around their waists will begin a dance.

If a man has died, these will be his sisters. If he had no sisters, they will be close relatives. If it was a woman who died, these women who dance will be the sisters of the husband. A drummer will be standing in a stationary position and the women will dance in a circle around him. They will not sing. This dance will continue for about ten minutes, and then the leaf-skirted dancers will slowly and gradually start moving the dance closer and closer to the guest hut where the bereaved spouse has been waiting until then. The arrival of these women dancers at the doorway of the guest hut signals the start of the ceremony which constitutes the official termination of the mourning period which the spouse has undergone since the man's (or woman's) death.

## F.   END OF THE MOURNING PERIOD.

The public act of burning the *igiya* (the rope cord that a widow or widower ties around the waist on the day that the spouse dies) constitutes the official end of the mourning period. There is a ceremony of secondary importance which precedes this one and that consists of the cutting of the bereaved person's hair before the removal and burning *igiya*.

When the women wearing the leaf skirts reach the guest hut the person who has been waiting inside comes out to meet them. The dancers escort him (her) to the place where the *igiya* will be removed and burned. They will follow the main path from the compound until it is intersected by another, i. e. until a cross road is reached. The ceremony will be performed at this intersection. As they process from the guest hut to the intersection, the drummers (who have not stopped beating their drums since the women started their dance) will be in the lead, followed by the widow (widower) who is being escorted by the women who have just finished their dance, and then by most of the remaining people. While they are walking to the spot (they are no longer doing the slow shuffle dance) some people will be singing the *wak'ar gormo* — the particular song that the husband sang when he was courting his wife. If a husband has died, the song will be sung in remembrance of him; if the wife died, it will be sung in remembrance of she to whom it was sung.

When the procession arrives at the place where the main path is intersected by another, the first thing that is done is the preliminary ceremony of shaving the widower's or widow's head.[5] This is usually done by one of the elderly women — both for men and women. The woman first washes the person's head (merely to soften the hair for the shaving, not with any symbolic meaning).

Then the hair is shaved off with either a razorblade or a very sharp knife, and all of the hair is collected in a calabash. Into another calabash, which contains the water that was used for washing the person's head, people will drop donations of money, usually a penny or three pence. This money will be given to the old woman who has performed the head shaving. When the person's head is completely shaved and all the hair has been collected into the calabash, a close relative of the deceased will be chosen to take the hair and dispose of it in the bush. A female relative will be chosen if it was a woman's head that was shaved; a male relative will dispose of a man's hair. The place where the hair is deposited is supposed to be unknown to anyone except the person who disposes of it.[6]

When the head-shaving and disposal of the hair have been completed, the time has come for the main ceremony — the burning of the *igiya*. One man will have been delegated to remove this cord from the waist of a widower; a woman will be chosen to remove it from the waist of a widow. A small amount of dry grass is placed on the path — exactly where the two paths intersect — and the *igiya* is put on top of the grass. Then the grass is set on fire and burns until the *igiya* is completely burnt to ashes. These ashes are then carefully gathered in a calabash and disposed of in the same manner that the hair was. When the person who disposes of these ashes returns to the group, the ceremony is thereby regarded as being concluded. . . the mourning period is at an end. This is the "official" end of the Funeral *Biki* although general dancing and socializing will continue for another day and a half.

---

[5] There will, of course, be very little hair on a widow's head, which will repeatedly have been shaven during the mourning period. See pp. 141, 145 and 147 *supra*. *(Ed.)*

[6] This is, of course, an almost universal custom in Hausaland, and is intended to avoid the possibility of *maita* (witchcraft), utilizing parts of the intended victim's body that have been carelessly or unwittingly made available to the witch or warlock. *(Ed.)*

If the widower, or widow, plans to remarry, a one month interval will have to be observed, from the day that the mourning period ended until the day on which the marriage is to take place. The most likely example of this would be of a widow marrying her former husband's younger brother (if they lived in the same compound) so that she would not have to return to her parent's compound. She would not be permitted to remain for any length of time if she did not remarry.

## CHAPTER TWELVE

# OTHER FESTIVALS

## A.  GENERAL DESCRIPTION

In an earlier chapter, a simple overall description of a *biki* was given as "a social event when Dukkawa — men, women, and children — gather together for one or more days of dancing, singing and drinking." Apart from the last chapter on Death — where the Funeral *Biki* is intimately and inextricably associated with the Dukku beliefs and customs concerning mortality, there have been several occasions when a *biki* has been referred to, but where full explanation has been deferred. The reason for this is simple enough; *biki* occupy a unique place in the Dukku pattern of life and, as such, they deserve detailed consideration apart from the various particular facets of life to which they are conjoined.

The unique aspect of a *biki* is that it is the *main* social activity for the Dukkawa. And, for all practical purposes, it is the *only* really social activity. There is a certain social aspect to the marketplace — and occasionally men will go there just to drink and to converse — but there is almost always an economic aspect as well. Hunting trips are, in a certain sense, social events but the social aspect is certainly not the primary purpose for leaving on an expedition.

There are various kinds of *biki* called for by specific occurrences — e. g. marriage, death — and although attendance at these is necessitated (more or less, depending upon the importance of the occasion) as an observance of Dukku tradition, still the main reason that people go there is to see their friends, exchange gossip, or just to have a good time.

155

The general arrangement of people at these *biki* is in small groups of ten or fifteen. Men will sit together, women will assemble apart. The people tend to group themselves according to age groups (naturally so, if they are going to talk about things of common interest) or according to particular occupations, e. g. hunters, blacksmiths. These are not definitive groupings to which a person will remain attached for the entire duration of the *biki*. Anyone is free to move around from group to group as he wishes. But in every group there is someone who has precedence, usually determined by age. Whenever food or drink is brought to the group by the women of the compound where the *biki* is being conducted, it will be brought to this person. He, in turn, will portion things out to those assembled in his group.

The singing which accompanies most of the different kinds of dancing at the various kinds of *biki* is not characterized by any wide range of variation in tempo and melody. Not much variation can be expected when the only accompanying instrument is a drum, nor when the tempo of the singing must be in balance with the tempo of dancing which is generally of a similar style in most cases.

But Dukku singing at these *biki* is characterized by its lyrical content. There are particular songs for every occasion, as well as particular songs for specific groups at the same occasion. Men and women each have their collection of traditional songs. Some are sung only by older men, others by younger men, while some are sung only by unmarried men making *gormo,* etc. The same is true for women's songs. In the modern musical field, songs are generally divided into "golden oldies" and "new hits." There are no "new hits" among the Dukkawa; all the songs sung at *biki* are "golden oldies"; traditional chants. For example, it is not a matter of someone composing a new song for a Funeral *Biki.* As one Dukku man explained when asked about the possibility of new songs, "It is not that we are against new songs as much as it is expected that the old songs be sung."

Dancing is ordinarily associated with festive occasions, "festive" in the sense of times of joy and happiness. If you have learned that someone's mother just died, for example, you do not immediately approach the person and say "Let's go dancing!" Although most of the Dukku *biki* are festive occasions, it is however a fact that the Funeral *Biki* is almost continuous dancing from beginning to end.[1]

Dancing, for Dukkawa, is simply the *physical expression of a particular sentiment sensed on a specific occasion.* This is, indeed, precisely the same principle which forms the basis of ballet. By appropriate dancing, a person can outwardly manifest his interior sentiments of sorrow just as easily as he can adapt his physical gestures to manifest happiness or joy.[2]

As just mentioned above, all singing and most dancing at Dukku *biki* is done to the accompaniment of *drums.* There are five different kinds of drums which are used interchangeably, although sometimes a particular type of drum must be used for a specific type of dance or for a particular group of dancers. Before considering the different kinds of *biki*, it is well to present a fuller description of these drums and point out any particular usages of them. (Fig. 36).

1. *Ganga.* This is the largest of the five kinds of drums. It has a long cord or rope strap which the drummer slips his head through, positioning the *ganga* off his left hip. The drum is struck with a stick which is curved at the end so that it is almost perpendicular to the handle. This drumming-stick is flattened at the end which strikes the drum. While the drummer is striking the drum with the drumming-stick held in his right hand, he is also balancing the tempo by various beats with his left hand (not with a stick). There are different sizes of *gangas* between two and two and a half feet in length, and an average diameter of sixteen to eighteen inches. There are skins at each end, fastened along the sides with ropes which are bound two-by-two at the mid-section to keep them taut. Two or

---

[1] I remember the first time I attended a Funeral *Biki* and thought, "Isn't it peculiar that they are dancing at a time like this."

[2] There is an element of *sacrament* (an outward show of inward or spiritual emotion in this case) in all African Dance, which almost invariably has "social" connotations. In this, it differs from ballet in that in this medium, the artists are *performing,* the depth of their emotive talent notwithstanding. At, for example, a funeral *biki,* a BaDukku dancing is interpreting genuine (as opposed to assumed) emotion through his responses to the rhythm. *(Ed.)*

Fig. 36. Three of the five drums used by the Dukkawa.

three thin strings will be drawn — off center — across the skin to provide resonance. (See Fig. 37).

The *ganga* is the most frequently used of the drums. It will be used for almost all of the men's and boy's dances. It is also the drum used to announce the death of a person (as described in the last chapter), or to signal the opening of a *biki*. Except for these latter two instances, the *ganga* is almost never used except for dancing.

2.  *Kimba*. This is a long, narrow drum — three feet long with a nine to twelve inch diameter — which is closed only at one end. It is usually beaten with both hands from a sitting position. It is used specifically for the dances of young women. The skin covering, like that of the *ganga* and all the other kinds of drums, is either goat,

sheep, or duiker skin. It is fastened along the side of the drum with the same kind of ropes which are fastened around the *ganga*. There are no resonance cords drawn across the skin. (See Fig. 37).

The name of this drum — *kimba* — is worth noting. All Dukkawa use this name in describing this particular kind of drum. However, the Hausa dictionary does not refer to any kind of a drum under the word *kimba*. Actually,

Fig. 37. A *ganga* drum, with a *kimba* drum in the left foreground.

*kimba* is a kind of long, thin black pepper[3], about the size and shape of a person's index finger. Due to the similarity in shape it is suspected that the name of this drum has been awarded by analogy.

3. *Turu.* One of the particular types of *biki* which the Dukkawa have is the Hunters' *Biki* — which will be described in the next section of this chapter. It is held after the hunters return from a successful hunt. The various dances that the hunters perform will be done to the accompaniment of a drum called *turu*. The dances at this Hunters' *Biki* are not to be confused with the dance that hunters do at a Funeral *Biki*, in remembrance of a hunter who died. Such a dance at a Funeral *Biki* is led by the *ganga* drum.

The *turu* is a large drum (about three feet) which stands on a base. The skin is about fifteen inches in diameter and has two or three thin resonance cords drawn across it. Sometimes this drum is cradled under the arm, but — because of its size and weight, it is usually stood up on the ground and the drummer beats with both hands from a sitting position. It is hard to avoid an analogy with a kettledrum. (See Fig. 38).

4. *Kurkutu.* This is the smallest of all the drums, being about twelve to fifteen inches in height and ten inches across the diameter of the skin. Like the *turu,* although much smaller, the base is wood and it is played from a sitting position on the ground. Unlike the *turu,* which is played by hand, two sticks (straight, not curved like the drummingstick for the *ganga*) are used to beat the *kurkutu.* Also unlike the *turu,* there are no resonance cords drawn across the skin. (Fig. 38).

The specific use of this drum is at the Mai-Giro *Biki*, a religious gathering which will be fully described in the chapter on Religion. It is also sometimes used by individual groups at other forms of *biki* when their particular group wants accompaniment to sing songs (not, however,

---

[3] Xylopia Aethiopica, the African (also called Negro or Guinea) Pepper. This is a most pleasantly pungent pepper which is greatly esteemed. *(Ed.)*

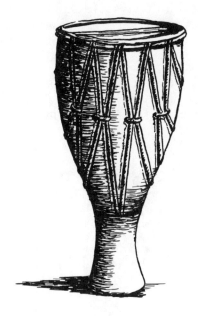

*Turu* drum

*Kurkutu* drum

Fig. 38. The *turu* and *kurkutu* drums.

with dancing). This small drum is sufficient for their purpose: loud enough for the group to hear, but not so loud as to distract from the main drumming and dancing that is going on at the time.

5. *Kalangu*. This is the widely known hour-glass drum which is popular throughout northern Nigeria. It is not a typically Dukku instrument, in fact there are[4] no ceremonial

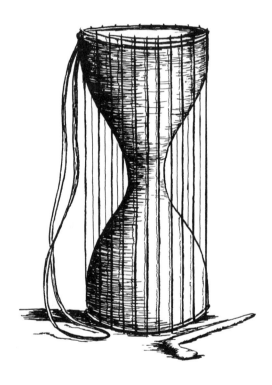

Fig. 39. The *kalangu* drum. Squeezing the cords alters the pitch.

---

[4] All of the drums listed are, in fact universally used throughout Hausaland, and the fact that various Dukku ceremonies give pride of place to specific instruments must not be taken as being presumptive of any "proprietary" or "inventive" rights! *(Ed.)*

dances at any of the *biki* in which this drum is used, although a few Dukkawa own them. The drum itself is an hour-glass shape, and its uniqueness is that it is strung all the way around, from top to bottom, with taut cords. The drum is closed at both ends and is struck with the *ganga*. When it is played, it is cradled against the side of the body with one arm. While it is being struck with the drumstick, the arm holding the *kalangu* is squeezed back and forth against the cords, producing a dual effect of drumming and strumming and varying the pitch. The *kalangu* is about two feet long and ten inches across the diameter of the skins. (Fig. 39).

## B. KINDS OF BIKI.

I. *Major biki*. There are three which the Dukkawa call "big" both in the sense that they are special commemorative occasions as well as from the fact that, as such, they demand more elaborate preparation.

1. Funeral *Biki*. In the last chapter, where this *biki* was described, it was pointed out that this is the only one of all the different kinds of *biki* which is obligatory for every married adult, or for an adult who had been married. This categorization would certainly include every Dukku man over twentyfive years old — at least, and every woman over twenty. A Funeral *Biki* is just as necessary for a woman as it is for a man.

   As mentioned, also, it is the obligation of the eldest son to arrange the father's *Biki*, and a husband's obligation to arrange his wife's. This is as far as the strict obligations are concerned, but it is very common that all of the male children of the deceased-individually, and at different times — will feel a necessity to arrange a Funeral *Biki* for their deceased parent. — One Funeral *Biki* attended was that which a Dukku man had arranged for his mother. As a result, it was thought that she had been living elsewhere. The man, however, disclosed that his mother had died fifteen years previously when he was only a small boy. He

had, he said, always had the thought in his mind that he
should do this thing for her.[5]

2. The Head-Farmer's *Biki*. It is necessary first of all, to explain this idea of Head-Farmer. It is strictly an honorary
title; it implies no authority or dominance of any kind
over the farmers.[6] It is simply a matter of prestige. Also,
it is not a title which other farmers bestow on a particular
man, or something he earns for himself in the sense that
he is a definitely superior farmer . . . . as is the case with a
*Sarkin Daji*, i. e. King of the Bush, who is accorded this
title by the people for his special prowess at hunting. The
title of *Sarkin Noma* — Head-Farmer — is taken by the
man himself if he wants to and if he can afford it.[7]

The Head-Farmer's *Biki* is the social gathering and celebration at which a man is officially recognized as a Head-
Farmer. In over nine years experience with the Dukkawa
in the area where this survey took place, there has only
been one Head-Farmer's Biki. And, among all the Dukkawa in this area, there are only three men who have the
title of Head-Farmer. So this particular *biki* is certainly
not a frequent occurrence. Yet it does have the necessary
traditional prestige which makes it a major occasion.

The main reason that it is a rare occurrence is that it is
very expensive for the person who is seeking the title,
since he alone has to assume all the financial burden. In
all, it will cost him about two hundred bundles of guinea-
corn. The price of a bundle of guinea-corn varies during
the year, according to its availability. It generally ranges
between five shillings a bundle — when it is very plentiful
right after the harvest season — to as high as ten shillings

[5] It must be observed that there is a clear element of that same "justifiable ostenta-
tion" to a Dukku *biki* that can be discerned in a *potlach* among the American Indians of
the North-West. *(Ed.)*

[6] Within the rigid framework of "legitimacy" and "deference" in African social
structure, it could be argued that there is no such thing as a "strictly honorary title". I,
indeed, would argue that *all* titles have their obligation and also their "pay-off". *(Ed.)*

[7] Many examples of "title taking" can be seen in other groups (e. g. the Ibo and the
title *Mazi*). However, there are sanctions on their being taken, and an aspirant for such
who was considered "unworthy" not only probably would not get very far in the process,
but might even hesitate to try for it at all. *(Ed.)*

during the Rainy Season when the previous year's supply is becoming depleted and the harvest has not yet begun. But even if the cheapest price is taken at six shillings a bundle, two hundred bundles of guinea-corn would be equivalent to sixty pounds or more than $150. From what has previously been mentioned about the Dukku economy, it is surprising that *any* Dukku man could afford to become a *Sarkin Noma!* And even more surprising that any would want to, since they receive nothing in exchange except a title. Yet, it is a traditional Dukku custom, and for a people who have nothing else, a title such as this is something to live one's life hoping for.[8]

There are two payments of guinea-corn, each of one hundred bundles. The man gives one hundred bundles of guinea-corn to the tax collector for the area. On the day of the *Biki* this tax-collector will present the new — Head-Farmer — with a turban as a sign of official recognition of his new status.[9]

The other one hundred bundles of guinea-corn will be given to a blacksmith who, in turn will make a special iron staff which is symbolic of the honorary office of the *Sarkin Noma.* This staff, like the turban, will be presented to the man on the day of the *biki.*

The staff itself is about five feet in length and pointed like a spear at the tip. About twelve or fifteen inches from the top there is a round knob, and just above this knob there is a curved metal projection. This staff is especially made in this way so that anyone seeing it well immediately know its owner is a *Sarkin Noma.* (See Fig. 40).

After his *biki,* the Head-Farmer can wear his turban and carry his special staff whenever he goes to market or to another *biki.* They seldom do this, however, (except possibly for a Funeral *Biki*) being content with the know-

[8] Regretfully, almost no research has been undertaken into the almost limitless field which traditional "Guild" titles such as that of a *Sarkin Noma,* a *Sarkin Daji,* a *Sarkin Fawa* etc., etc. offer. *(Ed.)*

[9] It must be pointed out that the official described here as the tax-collector, would be the District Head, the local Government Official for the area. *(Ed.)*

Fig. 40. Sketch of the Staff of Office of a *Sarkin Noma.*

ledge that everyone realizes they possess the status of
*Sarkin Noma.* There is also another very understandable
reason why they are not seen with their turban and staff
at the marketplace or at *biki.* The fact is that by the time
a man can save enough guinea-corn to seek the title — for
the few who reach that goal — they are usually very old
men who never go to market anyway and only seldom to
*biki.*[10]

3. *Marriage Biki.* Among the Dukkawa, this *biki* is considered to be the biggest celebration of all. Although it is
   only one and a half days in length from one evening
   through the following night — there is almost continuous
   festivity. As one Dukku man who was going to a Marriage

---

[10] Some doubt has been expressed as to the motive of "title taking" as in the
case described. There are, however, Western analogies. A countrybred Englishman would
have no difficulty in recognising the immediate similarity in effect of the title *Sarkin
Noma* and the English honorific M.F.H. (Master of Fox Hounds), a distinction so prized
that its owner employs it as if it were a decoration, *preceding* mere Academic Degrees.
The status of M.F.H. is purely honorary; it will cost its owner very large sums of money
indeed each year; it confers no authority at all beyond the immediate members of a
particular Hunt, but it conveys enormous prestige, and its mere appearance on a calling
card opens innumerable doors which would otherwise be closed, just as does the *Sarkin
Noma's* staff. Indeed, both represent the ultimate in elite status, one among the Dukkawa, and the other among the fox-hunting squirearchy! Perhaps it takes one traditional
society to recognise the foibles of another!! *(Ed.)*

*Biki* observed, "I will not sleep until the day after tomorrow."

The dancing begins on the first evening and continues throughout the night almost until sunrise. There is a break in the activity in the early morning hours for those who want to rest or sleep, and the drumming starts again about eleven o'clock and continues through the day and far into the night . . . . as long as the people can still dance.

*Preparation.* The new husband is responsible for all the preparations. Since many people will be coming, and he wants to provide the best of everything in abundance for this "once in a lifetime" event, it will take him about two months of continuous organization before he has things as he wants them. Since the man to be married is still young, he usually does not have a lot of money available and the cost of the *biki* will throw strain on him. He can expect to get financial help from his friends, especially those young men who were making *gormo* — farm work for the future father-in-law as dowry payment — at the same time that he was. Just as we saw that those making *gormo* will help each other with the farm work when each one's time comes, so will they help finance each other when it comes time to prepare for the marriage *Biki.*

Eight or ten men will come forward with five or ten shillings apiece, but this is still a very inadequate sum with which to prepare for the kind of Marriage *Biki* that every man wants to have. The Dukkawa estimate that at least twenty pounds (over fifty dollars) is needed to make a decent celebration. This is quite a sum for a young man around twenty years of age who has never done anything except work his father's farm. As a result, for several months before the date of the Marriage *Biki* the man will work at any odd-jobs he can find — usually farming, since that is all he really knows — in order to augment his finances.

If he cannot find work, he will make things — small wooden stools, hoe and axe handles, mats, rope, etc. — to sell in the market. — The man himself — not his parents, or the parents of the girl — will set the date for the Marriage *Biki.* Once the day is set, it will never be postponed. The usual time of the year for this occasion is either during *Bazara* — the last month of the Hot Season (May) just before the rains begin — or early part of the Rainy Season (June, July).

Invitations to the Marriage *Biki* will be made by the parents of the boy and the parents of the girl, as well as by the boy and the girl themselves. These invitations are given informally at the marketplace or anywhere that people happen to be met. For this singular occasion, the couple to be married would always wish for as many as possible to come to the *biki.*

The Marriage *Biki* is always held at the husband's compound, since this is the whole symbolism of the ceremony — i. e. the girl is officially leaving her parents' house to take up permanent residence with her husband.

On the day of the Marriage *Biki,* the one person who does not come to the celebration is the father of the girl. The reason for this is *kunya* — that special sense of modesty arising out of the special relationship which always results from particular degrees of intimacy between two people. Even the girl's mother will be somewhat restricted by this *kunya.* Usually she will not attend the festivities on the first night of the *biki* and will only arrive unobtrusively on the morning of the next day when the drumming and dancing and singing are in full progress.

There will be a Master of Ceremonies for a Marriage *Biki.* The father of the boy will choose one from among his close friends. This man will not give any speeches or have any official rituals to perform. His main function is to remain close to the boy's father and share the special joy of the occasion with him. The boy's father and the M. C. will usually sit on a *tabarma* — a grass mat — at some prominent location near the entrance to the compound in order to greet everyone who arrives, and to be greeted by them in turn. If anyone brings gifts, which many people do, they will be shown to the father and the M. C. who will make appropriate observations and agree how nice they are. For a Dukku man, there could be nothing more important than the marriage of one of his sons.

*Arrival of the bride.* A Marriage *Biki* begins in the late afternoon or evening. But earlier in the day the bride will leave her parents' compound and go to another compound in the near vicinity of her husband's — but *not* to his compound. The place to which she goes is that where one of her special girlfriends lives. During the remainder of the day other young women will also gather at that compound, and together with the girl they will prepare and arrange the different items that the bride will take with her to her new home.

This gathering of young women — up to about fifteen in number — constitutes the bridal party. They will remain together in the compound until after sunset, usually well into the night, before they depart for the husband's compound. It is the customary practice for this bridal party to "bring" the bride to her new home. As they move on their way, they are laughing and singing in unison, and their arrival at the *biki* itself is immediately noted by the others who have, of course, been expecting them to come.

The women go directly to a hut that has been prepared for them and seclude themselves inside while word is spread among the people outside that the bride has arrived. This causes a general stepping up of activity; the drumming is increased, more people move into the dances, and the groom and the groom's father are again congratulated on all sides, etc.

The bridal troup will stay with the girl during the entire time of the *biki*. Later that first night they will go out to dance and join the festivity, and then return to the hut. Food is brought to them the following morning by the husband's mother, or by one of his sisters, and the women will eat together inside the hut. Later they will again join in the celebrations.

*Gifts.* The husband must bear the expenses for the preparation of the Marriage *Biki*. This will include buying the meat and fish to feed all the people who will come, and guinea-corn both for food and for beer, as well as money to be given as gifts to relatives of the wife's family.

Though the husband's expenses pertain only to the preparation of the Marriage *Biki,* the girl's family has its financial burdens as well in providing gifts. Most of these gifts will be for their daughter and are presented to her towards the end of the *biki.* Some of the gifts will be for the girl's personal use, to aid in setting up her new household; others will be given to her friends and friends of her husband's or his family members as mementos of the day.

The following listing of gifts given to the bride by her family were observed at one particular Marriage *Biki.* They can be regarded as standard gifts which are given at virtually every Marriage *Biki,* although the number might vary slightly from *biki* to *biki.*

a. A mortar and pestle (for the girl's own use)
b. Three small wooden stools — which women use when working around the compound (one of these might be given to a special girl friend)
c. Two tin bowls (for the girl's personal use)
d. One pair of sandals
e. Two yards of cloth
f. A head scarf
g. A portmanteau (storage box) — for keeping personal items
h. Thirty clay pots (to be given to friends)
i. One hundred calabashes (to be given to friends)
j. Fifty calabash-spoons — small calabashes cut lengthwise (to be given to friends)
k. Seventy measures of guinea-corn (to be given to the husband's family to supplement the provisions for the people who have come to the marriage *Biki*)
l. Four large pots — each containing about four gallons — of guinea-corn beer (again, to be given to the husband's family to supplement the beer provided for the people attending the *biki*)

All of the above-mentioned gifts will be prepared by the girl's family and will be given to the girl, who will dispose of them according to custom. See Figure 41.

Fig. 41. Women with their gifts gathering for a Marriage *Biki*

Besides the gifts which the girl's parents are expected to provide, there are also voluntary gifts which the friends of the groom will give the man (or to his father). Most of these will be practical items, especially foodstuffs, which the husband will keep for the use of his family — unless they are in abundance, in which case he will portion them out among his relatives or his wife's relatives. The only exception to this is in the case of money. Money will almost always be given to the husband's father. When the Marriage *Biki* is nearly finished — after everyone has arrived and anyone who is going to offer money has already done so — the groom's father will give some money to each of the young women in the wife's bridal party; the remainder will be given to the bride's mother.

The usual gifts which friends of the groom bring are grass mats, soap, salt, peppers, onions, oil, meat, and fish. An especially close friend of the groom might give him a sheep or a goat.

Such, in brief outline, are the principal observances at the three "big" *biki*. To the casual visitor there would appear to be little difference between them. They are all large social gatherings — almost all the people from the area will attend — and the dancing and singing at each of them would seem to be very similar, at least to anyone who was not familiar with what was going on.

And yet there can be noted important characteristic distinctions which pertain to the various occasions: the multiplicity of ceremonial dances and the burning of the *igiya* at the Funeral *Biki;* the special significance of the turban and the staff at the *Bikin Noma* — the Head Farmer's *Biki;* the bridal party's ceremonial escorting of the bride to her new home and the multitude of gifts that are presented at the time of the Marriage *Biki*.

II. *Minor biki.* When considering *biki,* it should always be remembered that they are basically social gatherings at which singing and dancing and drinking are the main activities (Fig. 42). Sometimes there is a very special reason for such assemblies, such as the marriage or death of a person. But at other times, the reason for arranging a *biki* may not be so grave. In other words, for any particular reason, a man might decide to have such a social gathering at his compound. Depending on the importance that the person attaches to the reason for the *biki,* people from the entire area might be invited, or maybe just people within the immediate vicinity of the man's compound.

In this sense, it would be impossible to mention all the different kinds of *biki* that might conceivably arise, just as it would be an almost *ad infinitum* task to probe all the possible reasons a person might conjure up to call such a *biki*. But this is not necessary for our purposes, since this type of *biki* would all run to the same pattern and there would be no ceremonial dances or special rites attached to them. It would simply be a matter of getting-together to acknowledge or celebrate some particular event.

However, there are several *biki* which, although not of the same magnitude as the three already described, *do* have a special significance among the Dukkawa and therefore are conducted according to specific patterns.

1. *Mai-Giro Biki. Mai-Giro* is the special spirit to whom the Dukkawa pray, and once a year they gather together for a

Fig. 42. "Mulling" beer — Dukku fashion! Hot stones, taken from the fire, being dropped into *giya* to warm it.

ritual *biki* in his honor. Before considering this *biki*, it would be better to have a more definite idea of the Dukku ideas concerning spirits, and especially this main spirit *Mai-Giro*. A detailed description of the *biki* will therefore be deferred until the final chapter on Religion.

2. *Bikin Shanu* — the festival of the cow. This *biki* is so called because anyone who desires an "honorary share" of the actual authority or prestige possessed by another person will make the payment of one cow to that person. (For example, to a tax-collector — which is the most frequent instance of this kind of *biki*). In return for the cow, the person of authority or special prestige — e. g.

tax-collector — will prepare a *biki* for the person request-
ing it. On the day of the *biki* the man who made the payment of the cow will receive a new gown from the particular person he has chosen to arrange the *biki* for him, as
well as some cloth for his wife, and some other personal
items. He will also receive some sort of symbolic gift pertaining to the office or position which the other man
actually possesses. For example, a tax-collector might
give the man a turban, or a specially made leather bag, or
anything else which he feels commensurate to his position. There is nothing specified as to the exact nature of
the gift which is presented except that it must be considered to bespeak the office of the man.

The *Bikin Shanu* is not a frequent occurrence, although
the Dukkawa say that in years past it was done more
often. As is the case with the *Bikin Noma* — Head-Farmers
*Biki* — it is strictly a matter of prestige with no rights or
privileges attached.[11]

3. *Bikin Maharba* — Hunters' *Biki*. This gathering will be
collectively arranged by a group of hunters who have had
a successful hunting trip. They will share the expenses
equally, a cost which usually amounts to the price of
enough guinea-corn to make beer, since this is not an
elaborate *biki* and only lasts from one evening until the
following morning. The main purpose of the Hunters'
*Biki* is to invite other people to rejoice with them at their
good fortune.

The *biki* will begin about five o'clock in the afternoon
and the remaining hours before sunset will be spent in
"play acting" different aspects of the hunt. One man will

[11] The Colonial Government frowned upon it! It is but a short step from "assum-
ing" a part of, say, a tax-collector's "prestige" and utilising that "assumption" on one's
own behalf. This is, of course, a criminal offence, known in Hausa as *"sojan gona"* (soldier
of the farm) and describes the circumstances under which someone with a badge or a
cast off Army jacket etc. would batten on the unsuspecting peasantry and suck them
dry. In the (correct) displeasure which this invoked among Administrative Officers, it
is nonetheless the Editor's opinion that some traditional observances which were either
innocuous or, even, of value, came under the ban, which was stupid. In such cases, the
baby was thrown out with the bath-water! *(Ed.)*

Fig. 43. Dance in honor of the return from a successful hunt. The head on the left is that of a West African hartebeest, Bulbalis Major, *(kanki)* and that on the right of a bush-cow *(b'auna)*.

take the horns of one of the animals that was killed and put them on top of his head; another man will use two crossed sticks to represent a bow and arrow. The first man, to the accompaniment of drumming, will dance around the compound, in between the huts, etc. The "hunter" will stealthily move after him to make the "kill". Then the first man will run off somewhere — usually inside the guest hut to "lie down and die" while the "hunter" follows his trail. When the "prey" is finally discovered, there is a loud cheer from all the people who are watching the enactment. Then the killing of another animal will be represented, and so on until it is too dark to continue. The rest of the night is spent dancing and drinking. (See Fig. 43).

## CHAPTER THIRTEEN

# RELIGION

Some introduction is necessary before any serious discussion of the religious aspect of Dukku life can be undertaken. Most people are reasonably familiar with religious beliefs and practices according to one or other (or even some) of the major world religious groups, Christianity, Islam, Judaism, etc., in all of which there exist basic sets of doctrine and then a further extrapolation of belief pertaining to those various doctrines. These religions all set forth a precise presentation of their dogmatic premises and of their moral prescriptions. For example, choose any ten Moslem men and ask them a few basic questions concerning their religious beliefs. The answer will be one in which a general agreement among them can be discerned.

This is not the case with the Dukkawa and *their* religious beliefs, and the reader will have been seriously misled if at the conclusion of this chapter, he still retains any idea that the "Dukku Religion" consists of this or that specific code of belief. There are some religious tenets which are generally accepted by all Dukkawa — e. g. that there is a God, or that man has a soul. There are also some which do not have such universal affirmation.

Furthermore, the simple affirmation of the *fact* (e. g. Are there evil spirits?) is a completely different consideration from the explanation of that fact (What are evil spirits?). The point to be noted is this: As far as the Dukkawa are concerned, in the matter of explaining the beliefs which they profess, it is very often simply a question of personal interpretation by each individual.

Therefore, in the following pages, whenever there was a unanimous agreement on a particular point, it will simply be stated as a fact. Whenever this unanimity is lacking, the various opinions will be noted — and these will be listed in order of precedence. In other words, the first opinion will be the one most frequently expressed by the Dukkawa; the second opinion will be less common; and so forth.

## A.    GENERAL NOTIONS.

There is a universal belief among Dukkawa in the *existence* of God. Furthermore, this belief is extended to the assertion that there is only *one* God. Basically, this is the God who made all things, who has a part in everything that happens, and who knows all things.[1]

God will also reward "good" people. This is mostly in reference to this life: that a good man will live in happiness and peace, and will have a sufficiency of the things he needs. There is also a general feeling — "feeling" is a better word than "belief" — that after death the soul of a good person will somehow be taken care of by God — although there is nothing specific about the kind of reward to be received. Actually, this is more of a negative notion than a positive one in that it is not so much concerned with receiving a particular reward as it is with being freed from any pain or suffering that might exist after death.

This is probably just an adaptation from the Dukku view of life itself. Since their lives are highly regulated and most luxuries are beyond their means, the Dukkawa are usually satisfied with the bare necessities of life. Their main concerns and worries pertain more to the avoidance of sickness, hunger, and pain than to the accumulation of "luxuries."

---

[1] In regard to God's omniscience, I have frequently used the following example. "On a night when there is no moon and it is absolutely dark — and all the fires in the compound have been extinguished — a man enters his hut and puts his mat across the doorway. He is all alone in the hut. He does not light a fire inside the hut, nor is there any kind of light at all. Does anybody know what he's doing inside his hut? " The answer is "No one can know." Then I add, "That's right, nobody knows what he might be doing in there. Even God does not know." An immediate response: "Oh, yes he does!" Only two men have ever accepted my suggestion that God did not know what was happening inside the hut, and I am sure they did so merely because they did not want to disagree with me. In both cases, this was immediately evident when other people in the group challenged their statements and they retracted them. One of these men even remarked to me, "You tried to fool me, didn't you?"

Most Dukkawa are absolutely certain that a bad person will somehow be punished by God. If he does not suffer in this life, God will do something to his spirit after death. They have no idea what the man will have to suffer, but there is no doubt at all that it will be impossible for the man to escape.

Except for the *Mai-Giro biki* when all of the people gather together, prayer is mostly a private affair for each individual.

There are two times during the year when the master of the compound will perform a prayer-service. Both of these services are in relation to the farming season; the first is before the planting is begun, the second is just prior to harvesting.

*Pre-planting:* When the first heavy rain falls, the master of the compound will call all of the people to assemble in the center of the compound. This includes the women and children as well as the men. When everyone is sitting down, the master of the house stands up and leads a brief prayer asking God to give them a plentiful crop and to keep the men healthy and strong so they can work well. While the man is saying the prayer, he holds a small calabash filled with guinea-corn seeds. As soon as this prayer is finished, the women and children will remain in the compound while the master of the compound and all the men go to the farm and plant the seed from the small calabash. No prayers are said nor is any sacrifice performed before or during the planting of these seeds.

*Pre-harvest:* This is a ritual service which the master of the compound performs by himself. When the time for harvesting to begin is close at hand, the master will go to the farm. He will take a fowl — usually a chicken — with him as well as some guinea-corn flour and a clay pot. When he gets to the farm (no particular spot) he will dig a hole and put the clay pot inside so that the lip of the pot is level with the ground. He places the guinea-corn flour next to the pot (not inside it). Then he kneels down and places the fowl above the pot and cuts its throat, allowing the blood to fall into the pot. While he is doing this, he asks God to give his family happiness and he prays especially for a good harvest. The man utters this prayer in his own words; there is no special formula to be recited.[2]

---

[2] The two prayer-services just described are according to the traditional Dukku custom. Most of the older men observe it. Although there is no reason to suspect otherwise, I cannot say for certain if all the younger men are faithful to these practices.

Next he rubs the fowl's blood around the entire inside of the pot and finishes by cleaning the fowl. The feathers are left on the ground; nothing special is done with them. The guinea-corn flour is also left on the ground, next to the blood-smeared pot, and the man then takes the fowl back to his compound where the women will cook it.

Some tribes have special huts prepared as shrines for religious worship, or they might have a designated place outside the compound where they have built a mud and stone altar for worship. Muslims living in the bush or outside of town, where it is not convenient to go to the mosque, will clear an area about ten or fifteen feet in diameter and encircle it with a single row of stones. This will be the place where they gather five times a day to say their prescribed prayers. The Kamberi, on the other hand, frequently have a small hut inside which there are a few special pots and feathers, etc. One of the older men in the compound is considered to be the prayer-leader and will enter the hut and offer special prayers for anyone who requests them.

Except for the *Mai-Giro* hut, which is reserved for a particular religious service which is held only once a year, there are no huts in any of the Dukku compounds which are specifically set aside for religious worship. But there are two particular places where a Dukku man may go to offer prayers.

1.  Some men have made a small shrine next to a particular large tree which is near their compound. It is a very simple affair and usually consists of just keeping one pot next to the tree for the very special occasion when the person wants to sacrifice a fowl — the blood of the fowl will be left in the pot. (See Fig. 44).

    Those Dukkawa who want to designate such a place especially for offering prayers will choose one of the following three kinds of trees for this purpose (not any tree will do):

    A.  Baobab Tree — *kuka* (Adansonia Digitata, (Ed.))
    B.  Tamarind Tree — *tsamiya* (Tamarindus Indica (Ed.))
    C.  Copaiba Balsam Tree — *maje* (Pardaniellia Oliveri).

    Places for prayer by the Dukkawa will not be found near any trees other than one of the three above.

Fig. 44. Private prayer site near a Dukku compound.

Sometimes an individual will just go to the place and say a prayer. Other times, for some special reason, he will make an offering. If he does so, it can be one of two things. The more solemn offering would be to sacrifice the blood of a fowl (the bird would be taken back to the compound to be eaten), or, as a lesser obligation, he may take a calabash of guinea-corn beer with him and, after making his prayer, will pour the beer onto the side of the tree.

The area around such a tree is known to be a place where prayers can be offered, but it is not considered to be an especially sacred place. Sometimes men gather under the shade of the tree — since it is always a large one it is therefore

usually one of the most shady areas around the compound —
and just converse, or they might even be found drinking there.

2.    The second place which is considered appropriate for the
      offering prayers is along the main path leading to and from
      the compound. The exact spot is either where the path is
      intersected by another path, or where the main path itself
      forks either to the right or left.
      This path intersection has already been referred to as a place
      of special ritual ceremony in the Funeral *Biki*. It is at this
      spot that the *igiya* is ceremonially burned, thus denoting the
      official termination of the mourning period.[3]

Chickens are the only animal used in sacrifice. Formerly
goats and sheep were also used for this purpose — the older Dukkawa insist on this — but gradually the custom developed (probably as much for economic reasons as any other) that a chicken
would be recognized as *the* sacrificial animal.

Realizing that the older Dukkawa dislike any changes in their
traditional customs, it was suggested to one elder that it was un-
fortunate that goats and sheep were not sacrificed any more, since
it would be a much more ceremonious affair. The simplicity of his
response was a stunning example of the wisdom that is popularly
regarded as the attribute of these elders!

> "Using chickens is best. Everyone can afford them and there
> is thus no bickering about whose sacrifice is the better."

There is no developed ancestor cult in the sense that there are
any ritualistic prayers or sacrifice to be observed in regards to
one's forebears. The Dukkawa generally feel that they should
"pray" to their ancestors, but this, in fact, simply means that they
should "think about" them out of a sense of gratitude.

Although a few Dukkawa say that they ask their ancestors
for happiness — nothing more specific than this — most people
feel that they cannot help their ancestors by praying for them, nor

---

[3] Except for the ceremony of burning the *igiya* at the Funeral *Biki*, I do not know
of any specific rites which are performed at either of these two shrine areas, i. e. trees
and path-intersections. These simply seem to be designated places where a person can go
to pray if he so wishes.

can their ancestors be of any practical benefit to their own earthly well-being (which is their primary concern). Death to them is a finality.

The majority of Dukkawa believe that a person's spirit will have some kind of existence after death — although some say that the spirit dies with the body. This existence in the after-life, however, cannot be affected or changed by another human being still alive in this world, e. g. by praying for the departed person.

Since they do not have very many positive ideas about what happens to a person after death — and, therefore, what happened to their ancestors — it is understandable that the Dukkawa do not rely too heavily on them for help in their everyday problems.

## B.   SPIRITS

The Dukkawa have a definite belief in spirits but it is quite unspecified and cannot be said to amount to a religious cult. There are no specific spirits associated with fertility, rainfall, or hunting, etc. Spirits can influence many aspects of human life, but particular roles are not assigned to individual spirits. The only distinction the Dukkawa make — other than God and *Mai-Giro* — are between good spirits and bad spirits.

All Dukkawa admit that *good* spirits exist. This universal assent is somewhat surprising when their views concerning the powers which the good spirits have are considered. Views indeed which are in almost diametrical opposition, though the first opinion is by far the most prevalent.

1. Good spirits simply exist but have no power to help a person in any way. They are called "good spirits" simply for the reason that they will not harm anyone.

2. Good spirits can sometimes prevent evil and suffering, e. g. snakebite or sickness. This is, however, strictly a preventative assistance.

Even according to this second opinion — and obviously in the case of first — no one seems to believe that good spirits have any positive influence in assisting a person to obtain something good which he is seeking.

If good are ineffectual — or relatively so — *bad* spirits most certainly are not. All Dukkawa are in agreement that bad spirits can cause sickness, cripple a person, and cause them to become mad (either temporarily or permanently). As to whether or not these bad spirits have the power to actually kill anyone, there are varying opinions.

1. They can kill a child, but not an adult.

2. They can kill either a child or an adult — an adult however, can safeguard himself if he uses the proper "medicine" (either a charm or some form of ritual purification).[4]

3. Bad spirits do not have the power to kill a person, only God can determine when a person is to die.

In any case, bad spirits are taken very seriously by the Dukkawa. What are bad spirits? Nobody knows, since they cannot be seen by human beings. "But, whatever they are, they can hurt you."

If you cannot see them, how are you sure they exist? In answer to this question, one of three answers is given.

1. Bad things happen to people and there is no natural explanation for them, e. g. a sane person starts acting irrationally. Something bad must have caused this effect, and since there is no (apparent) natural cause, it must be a *supernatural* cause. These are bad spirits!

2. Sometimes the wind is blowing . . . and the leaves on the trees are not moving.

3. Our forebears taught us about bad spirits, and they knew more about these things than we do.

Whether or not these reasons would be universally accepted as conclusive proof of the existence of bad spirits, they are more

---

[4] I stress *proper* "medicine" because sometimes people who have had "medicine" die from an unknown cause — which is frequently attributed to the bad spirits. The only explanation for this is that the "medicine" was not the right kind.

than sufficient authority for the vast majority of Dukkawa.

*Dwelling places of spirits.* Some Dukkawa say that they have no idea where spirits live, but most people have some definite opinions concerning were and how they do.

Do good and bad spirits live together in the same place? The opinions are divided almost equally: some say the two kinds of spirits live in the same places, others say they live separately.

Can spirits leave their dwelling places and travel? There is a general uncertainty as to whether good spirits travel or not. As for bad spirits, they definitely travel through the bush. Most Dukkawa do not think that these bad spirits will enter large towns or villages. People of other tribes living in towns would certainly disagree with this opinion!

As to the travelling that these bad spirits do, the following points should be noted:

1. Bad spirits will mostly travel at night, staying at their "home" during the day-time. During the day, therefore, a person can only be harmed if he ventures too close to the spirits' dwelling place.

2. There are certain kinds of bad spirits who are always travelling through the bush and have no permanent dwelling places. This certainly seems to destroy the relative security a person might feel during the day-time, as enunciated in the first opinion.

Where exactly do these spirits live? There is one place that was mentioned by almost every BaDukku who held that they had dwellings at all. Two other places were mentioned frequently enough to merit consideration also.

1. At the *base* of very large trees. Informants are very specific in pointing out that the "base" of the tree does not mean in, or around, the roots, nor inside the tree trunk. The spirits live on the ground, all around the circumference of the tree, immediately adjacent to the trunk.[5]

---

[5] It is worth recalling here that one of the places where religious shrines — simple as they might be — are set up is near *very large trees*. Not all large trees harbor bad spirits, so it is not a case of making a shrine where bad spirits live.

2. At the base of *large* rocks.

3. In *uncultivated* fields where no trees or shrubs are growing. Since trees and bushes and plants are all over the
   bush, it is understandable that the people would immediately think there is something sinister about a large
   open field where nothing is growing.

A bad spirit can cause rational people to become insane, but
once this occurs, it is not necessarily believed that the bad spirit
has possession of a person or that it permanently dwells in him.
Once a bad spirit makes a person insane, there is no further reason for the spirit to remain with him. The Dukkawa have no medicine to cure insanity. Generally, they just ignore the mad and
make sure they do not come close to the children.

Someone in the mad person's own family, however, might
offer a sacrifice to help him. As this affliction has just been described, it is not so much asking that the bad spirit be driven out
of the lunatic as it is of seeking a removal of the effect which the
bad spirit has caused. If a mad man does something bad, the action
is attributed to the person himself and not of any spirit that has
possession of him.

Although the Dukkawa do not believe that bad spirits take
permanent possession of a person, they do believe that a bad spirit
can control someone for a brief period of time. This, again, is
attributed to bad spirits because there is no apparent explanation
for the circumstances.

In such cases, the subject becomes very melancholic and
introverted, although there may be no danger that he will harm
anyone. This is not something which can happen to anyone at
random, but periodically it affects the same people. It is best explained in the words of a Dukku man who described the case of
his wife.

"She does not have this all the time. Once every two or three
months, for about an hour, she will begin shouting in a loud
voice and speaking some language I do not understand. She
does not walk around or try to harm anyone, she just goes
and sits in her hut and shouts things that I do not under-

stand. Even if someone went and sat next to her, I do not think there would be any danger. I just stay outside the hut until she finishes, and then everything is the same as before.''

Since the Dukkawa believe so strongly in the power of the bad spirits and the serious threat they pose to their happiness and safety, it is only natural that they should have devised means of protecting themselves from this evil effect. The most common means of protection is the wearing of charms which are believed to impede the evil designs of the bad spirits. Another means of protection against bad spirits is by some sort of ritual purification. This largely can be left to the individual, whatever he has found to be effective, but there is one purification which seems to be practiced by quite a few Dukkawa — not necessarily the majority of them, but a sufficient number of them to make it worth noting.

A fire will be made from the wood of a particular tree. A person, leaning over the fire, will put a cloth over his head and inhale the smoke. This smoke, inhaled into the lungs — and presumably retained there — is thought to ward off bad spirits. Those who observe this practice, perform such purification once or twice a month.

Two things are noteworthy about this procedure:

First,        — it cannot be smoke *per se* which is held to protect a person against bad spirits because this purification can only be accomplished by burning the wood of a certain type of tree.

Secondly,     — this process of purification against bad spirits is the very same process that was described earlier as a remedy for headaches and malaria. There is a difference, however, in that the wood used for the fire in curing headaches and malaria was specified as wood from the Frankinsense tree, whereas the wood for the ritualistic purification is not the same (name unknown).

## C.   CHARMS

Charms are objects possessing magical power. They can be used either for assistance in obtaining desirable things or as protection against harmful things. By Dukkawa they are employed for the following purposes:

a.   Special help to get good things
b.   Protection against bad things and bad people
c.   Special help for hunting different animals
d.   Protection against dangerous animals

Most Dukkawa wear charms. They can be worn around the waist (which is considered the most appropriate place) or they can be worn on leather cords — which themselves can also be charms — around the neck.

When attached to the cord around the neck, each particular charm is individually enclosed in a small leather packet — either rectangular or circular in shape (no special significance) —which is stitched around the sides. In most instances, at least for the charms the Dukkawa themselves make, the actual charm is a small amount of pounded tree bark.

The Dukkawa also occasionally purchase charms or some other representative symbols, from Moslem preachers (*Malamai*) which consist of a few words written in Arabic on a bit of paper. The piece of paper is then folded tightly and enclosed in a small leather case and stitched shut.[6] This second type of charm — the written charm — is usually sought for assistance in special cases. The individual seeking assistance will give a detailed description of the problem which is bothering him, and the mallam will prepare a specific remedy or assurance pertaining to the exact nature of the problem.

Before becoming too involved in a general description of these charms, and going on to a more detailed listing of the particular kinds of charms, there is one question which needs prior consideration. What significance do the Dukkawa attach to the charms which they wear?

---

[6] In Hausa these are known as *layu*. (Ed.)

It is an important question since a knowledge of the charms themselves gives no indication of their importance. Furthermore, it is a difficult question to determine at all with any degree of real accuracy since this is one instance when reliance can not be placed on the Dukkawa themselves to supply the answer. Granting their sincerity — which certainly must be taken for such in the case of the people questioned — there are frequent discrepancies between what they say and how they act.

It would be a very simple matter to accept the Dukkawa's own views concerning the value of charms, since they are about equally divided into two opposing opinions.

1. Charms definitely have power to assist a person towards good or away from evil.

2. Charms have no power and are only worn as decorations — a traditional custom of the Dukku tribe.

Although the two classifications are valid — i. e. those who believe in the power of charms, and those who do not — the difficulty lies in determining which people fall into which category.[7]

After long association with the Dukkawa and after close observance of their daily life, the following classification is offered, however, as providing a more accurate understanding of the people's attitudes towards charms:

1. There are those who say that charms are useful . . . and who manifest some degree of confidence in their power.

2. There are those who say that charms are useful . . . but manifest no reliance whatsoever in their supposed power.

3. There are those who say that charms are useless . . . and who do not possess any.

4. There are those who say that charms are useless . . . and who not only possess them, but will not part with them.

---

[7] It should also be pointed out that among those who are *pro* charms there are differences of opinion as to exactly how powerful their assistance really is, although no one believes they are absolutely infallible.

Many examples of the "contrary" cases could also be mentioned i. e. when a person says one thing and apparently believes the opposite[8] but a few suffice to illustrate the point. Each is an actual occurrence.

A.	Dogo has a charm which safeguards him against anyone wanting to hit him with a stick. The stick will either miss him completely or, if it does strike him, he will not be hurt. He was asked to close his eyes, after which an attempt would be made to hit him with a heavy tree branch.

His response was "No, this charm only works against other Dukkawa."

All right, there happens to be another Dukku man present, so let him be given the branch and the suggestion made that *he* hit Dogo.

Dogo's response was "No, this charm only works if another person is truly angry with me."

Rather than cause any breach of friendship between the two men, the matter was not pursued further!

B.	Previous conversation had been held with Kwara about the various charms he wore and their effectiveness. At the time, he explained that one of his most powerful charms was the one which protected him against snakes. Several people in his compound had been bitten by snakes, but it had never happened to him. Nor would he be afraid to approach a snake – any kind – and kill it.

Several months later it was learned that Kwara had been bitten by a snake, and accordingly a visit was paid to him (mainly to see if he required medical treatment – depending on the type of snake that bit him) and the conversation about his charm against snakebite was recalled.

Yes, he was wearing the charm when he was bitten! Yes, the charm is effective against all snakes.[9]

---

[8] Though in many cases, he himself does not realize this.

[9] I was surprised at both answers. If he had been wearing the charm, I was almost sure that he would say that this was the one kind of snake for which the charm was ineffective. I presumed so from similar conversations with other Dukkawa. Never having pre-

A suggestion was therefore made that it appeared that his charm was worthless. The answer was surprising. "No, I was not *thinking about* the charm when the snake bit me!" As it turned out, the charm is always one hundred percent effective . . . provided that you remember that you are protected by it. This was the first time that this particular rationalization was encountered.

C. Goro does not believe that charms are of any particular use. Formerly he had a few which he wore "because they look nice and because they had always been worn by Dukkawa." At the time of conversation, he had not worn charms for several years, nor did he own any. This statement was checked out with other members of his compound as well as with some of his close friends, and it was true. Then, however, there was a rumor that another man was interested in Goro's wife. The first thing Goro did was get a charm!

These three examples serve to point out the differences between professed belief and actual practice. It would be impossible to draw any valid inferences pertaining to the Dukkawa's exact beliefs concerning the value of charms, since the matter is basically a personal one and varies from individual to individual. Judging from circumstances and behaviour, the best that can be done is to approximate their general attitude towards charms. In formulating an opinion, the following criteria have been used:

1. Among any simple people — those who have no reason to question the causes of many of the events which enter their daily lives — it is natural that superstition should arise, for it is nothing else than the outcome of hypothetical conclusions, based on the few available facts.

2. The only really effective remedy for any disorder is one which is based on a precise understanding of the nature of the affliction.

---

viously met a BaDukku who would retract his original expressed conviction about the efficacy of a particular charm, my immediate reaction was "Well! There is a first time for everything!"

For example, a doctor will not prescribe a particular antidote for sickness until he has weighed all the symptoms
and determined the exact kind of disease he is dealing
with.

In the case of the Dukkawa's attitude towards the value
of charms, uncertainty is the basis of their hypothetical
conclusions — e. g. since there is no apparent explanation
for a misfortune, it most likely is the work of a bad spirit.
If the nature of the affliction is uncertain, the effectiveness of the remedy must be proportionately uncertain. In
other words, if they are not sure of what caused something, they are not sure whether a cure will work.

3.  The characteristics which the Dukkawa themselves have
    exhibited must be included. On the one hand, their gen-
    eral notions about God, spirits, and religion are very basic
    and simple. There are no detailed elaborations. On the
    other hand, the Dukkawa are a very practical people.[10]

In view of these three considerations, it can be concluded
that: —

1.  All Dukkawa have some regard for the possible effective-
    ness of charms.

2.  Very few Dukkawa seriously rely on this effectiveness.

If one had to summarize their attitude in one's own words, it
could be said:

"Charms might possibly help me, and I certainly cannot loose
anything by wearing them."

*Kinds of charms.* As has been implied in the discussion concerning the nature of charms, there can be a charm for almost anything. Most of the people make the commonly-used charms themselves since they are all familiar with the reputed antidote that
they are seeking. However, in special cases, when something extra-

---

[10]  A good example of this is the time I asked a Dukku man if he would get a charm
to cure his son from a sickness. He replied, "No, because we know the medicine — kind
of herbs — that will cure it. I only use charms when I do not know the medicine."

ordinary arises, it might be necessary to go to one of the elders in order to get his advice, or to have him make the charm.

The following is a listing of charms which are most commonly used, i. e. ones which most people have.

I. *For good things:*

1. *Farin jini* — white blood. This is the term used to describe popularity. The purpose of the charm is so that people will like you.[11]

2. *Farming.* (This was mentioned previously on the section on *gormo.*) This charm is supposed to strengthen a man to be a good farmer and to surpass all others at work.

3. *For women.* This charm is worn by a man so that women will like him.

4. *For the world.* This is an all-inclusive charm by which a person can find it easy to obtain anything that is good in the world.

II. *Against bad things:*

1. *Against sorcerers.* The Dukkawa have a particular belief about sorcerers which will be explained later.

2. *Against arrows, knives, and swords.* In general, this charm is protection against any kind of metal object which can be used to harm a person. Some say that the charm affects the metal itself and it will melt if the possessor has any ill intent against the person wearing the charm. Others say that the charm affects the arm of the person wielding the weapon, and he will not be able to lift it.

---

[11] The idioms *farin jini, bakin jini* etc. are not easy to explain. However, in some circumstances, *fari* (or *baki*) do not *mean* "white" (or "black") in any literal sense. They mean, rather, "well disposed" (or "ill disposed"). English has precisely the same usage — "I got nothing but black looks!", etc. It is true that the English only reflects one aspect, and does not, in modern usage at any rate, employ the full white/black dichotomy. However, c. f. the Latin *candidus* (white in complexion), from which derives "candid", meaning, *inter alia,* "frank", "sincere", as well as "outspoken". *(Ed.)*

3. *Against murder.* This seems to be another all inclusive charm which covers all the possibilities that were not covered by the previous charm.

4. *Against Bad Spirits.* This is a general charm against all bad spirits since, as mentioned earlier in this chapter, the Dukkawa do not attribute particular evil works to different bad spirits.

5. *Against wooden objects* (or objects that are partly wooden) e. g. an axe, matchet, etc.

III. *For good luck in hunting animals.*

The Dukkawa can have a charm for any animal they hunt, and therefore, the charms they most commonly use are for the animals they most commonly hunt or desire to kill.

| | |
|---|---|
| 1. Elephant | 6. Warthog |
| 2. Buffalo | 7. Kob |
| 3. Roan Antelope | 8. Reed buck |
| 4. Hartebeest | 9. Bush buck |
| 5. Waterbuck | 10. Oribi |

It should be noted that for hunting animals, there is usually a double charm. The first is the ordinary charm which is the pounded bark of a particular tree which is worn in a leather packet attached to a cord around the neck, or is somehow fastened onto the clothing. But a portion of this bark — different bark for different animals — will be mixed in, and cooked with, guineacorn porridge and then taken by the hunter before he leaves, on his hunt.

IV. *Against harmful animals.*

Again, there can be a charm for protection against any animal which is considered harmful, so the most common charms are those against animals which present the most frequent danger.

1. *Against snakes.* It is noteworthy that although the Dukkawa are familiar with the various types of snakes

in the area, and the ones which are more dangerous than others, they generally have only one charm which is supposed to be effective against all snakes.

2. *Against scorpions.*[12]

3. *Against warthogs.* This charm which is a protection from the tusks of this dangerous animal is a different kind from the charm which is supposed to bring luck in hunting warthogs.

Special mention has to be made about the Dukkawa's belief concerning sorcerers, since all Dukkawa seem to know about them and generally give the same explanation. It must be pointed out, however, that although there is unanimous agreement on what a sorcerer is and how he operates, no one with whom the question was discussed was able to point to an actual case in which a sorcerer had been involved. Only in one instance — the death of a small girl — has someone hinted that it might have been the work of a sorcerer.

The Dukku belief about sorcerers is that he, or she (it can be a woman just as well as a man), can cause the death of a person by giving that person human flesh to eat. It happens this way: A sorcerer will somehow "slip" a piece of human meat to his victim, unbeknown to him. (Where do they get the human meat? They unearth a recently buried body.)

After the victim has eaten the meat, the sorcerer will not mention anything about it until later, sometimes as long as a year or two afterwards. Then, he (she) will say, "Remember that meat I gave you on such and such a day? It was human flesh. Now I claim your spirit!" According to this belief, the Dukkawa hold that the sorcerer must then receive the spirit of the victim claimed.

---

[12] The belief in the efficacy of charms against scorpions *(kunama)* is so strong that they can be bought in any market. The charm is named *kamun kunama,* and in Sokoto market at any rate, its vendors are so confident of its powers that they offer a calabash containing perhaps fifty scorpions, into which the purchaser is invited to thrust his hand. Few do! The charms themselves are nothing more than brightly coloured bits of wool, to be tied round the arm. The Editor did, however, meet and know personally one man who had "power" over scorpions. He always had two or three on his person, usually on top of his shaven head, underneath his *tagiya* (="yarmulke") and they were NOT "defanged". (Ed.)

However, there are two ways out of this situation:

1. The person who ate the meat may make an agreement with the sorcerer to take the spirit of another person in his compound rather than his own, and the sorcerer will usually agree to this.

2. As soon as the person has been informed that he has eaten human meat, he can publicly "declare" the other person to be a sorcerer, and the latter's power will immediately be broken.

In reality, it seemed that thus there was no real danger since a public declaration removed the curse. However, almost all the Dukkawa questioned said that a person would almost never make such a declaration. The reason they gave was that once a person realised that he had eaten the flesh of another human being, which is considered a horrible thing to do, he would want to die!

From where does a sorcerer get his special power? He is born with it. But a sorcerer will not necessarily beget children with that same power. Two ordinary people may have a child who will become a sorcerer; equally, all of a sorcerer's children can be perfectly normal.

It appeared, therefore, that once a sorcerer had killed a person, he would immediately be detected, but this is not the case as the Dukkawa describe it. The sorcerer will remove the person's spirit and put it into the body of some animal (the victim will appear to be sleeping). Then the sorcerer will kill the animal and the person will die. Even if people are present, they will think the person died a natural death.

What is the purpose of the charms which are worn against the power of the sorcerer?

1. A person will be able to detect human meat if it is given to him.

2. It is a protection against having one's spirit given to a sorcerer by someone in the compound who has eaten human meat and who wants to transfer the debt to the second person (in which case he would know nothing about it at all).

## D.  MAI-GIRO

All of the Dukkawa say that *Mai-Giro* is "their Lord". He is the one spirit to whom they especially pray, and is considered as the special protector of the Dukku tribe. (Note: *Mai-Giro* is also considered the special protector of other tribes, e. g. Kamberi.)

Every BaDukku knows about *Mai Giro*. The question is: who is *Mai-Giro*?  It is surprising that for someone (something? ) which is so universally known, more than half the Dukkawa admit that they do not know who *Mai-Giro* is! From those who venture an opinion, the following conjectures arise:—

1. *Mai-Giro* is an especially powerful good spirit who is above all other good spirits, but not as powerful as God.[13]

2. *Mai-Giro* is just a special name for God. This is how the Dukkawa address God.

3. *Mai-Giro* is the spirit of a very good and powerful man who lived a long time ago..

Although the Dukkawa are quick to answer that *Mai Giro* is the one that they pray to, it remains that there is only one official gathering a year which is specifically assembled for this purpose.

At some time immediately preceding or following the harvest — between November and January — the elders will have a meeting and decide when the *Mai-Giro Biki* will take place. Then all the people will be notified. The only preparation for this *biki* is the making of guinea corn beer. The *Mai-Giro Biki* itself is a very short gathering, beginning in the late afternoon, around four o'clock, and finishing before sunset.

There is a special *Mai-Giro* hut in each general area where Dukkawa live. By "general area", an area of approximately five to eight square miles is intended. In the surveyed area, which is twenty miles from one end to the other, there are three *Mai-Giro* huts. These huts are just outside a particular man's compound.

---

[13] I have tried to determine if, in this sense, *Mai-Giro's* role is intercessory between the Dukkawa and God, but the people have no definite ideas on this.

There are three so-called offices associated with *Mai-Giro* worship. The Dukkawa themselves have no official names for these offices — they merely describe the function of each person's particular responsibility — so, in our terms, they can be called *headman, prayer leader* and *custodian of the Mai-Giro hut.*

1. *Head man.* This is the man who is responsible for *Mai-Giro* worship in the area. He is the one who is considered as the ultimate authority on *Mai-Giro.*

2. *Prayer-leader.* This is the man who officiates at the *Mai-Giro Biki.*

3. *Custodian of the Mai-Giro hut.* This is the man at whose compound the hut is located.

These three men are all reputable elders among the Dukkawa. The Head man is frequently the oldest Dukku man in the area. Sometimes these three offices are held by one person, i. e. the Head man will also be the prayer-leader at the *Mai-Giro Biki,* and the *Mai-Giro* hut will be just outside his compound. In other areas, three distinct men will hold the offices.

The *Mai Giro Biki.* When all of the people have gathered in the late afternoon, they will sit on the ground outside the *Mai-Giro* hut. The men will sit nearer the hut, and the women will be behind them. The prayer-leader will sit on a large stone just *outside* the doorway of the *Mai-Giro* hut, facing the people. He will call two other elders to come and sit next to him. Inside the hut, there will be a group of from six to ten elders sitting on the floor, and one of these men will be beating a small drum (there is no singing at any time during this *biki*).

The first thing on the agenda is the distribution of guinea-corn beer to everyone present. Once all the people have started drinking, the pray-leader will say a short prayer asking for God's blessing — there is no special formula for this prayer — and then he will appoint one of the two men sitting with him to kill the chickens which the people have brought.

Anyone who wants can bring a chicken. Even though all the Dukkawa in the area usually come for this *biki*, relatively few chickens are offered, however. The blood from these chickens is poured on the ground directly in front of the doorway — no prayer is said at this time. The chickens are then cooked and distributed to the people to be eaten, beginning with the elders.

This distribution is then followed by more beer drinking for an hour or two, and then everyone goes home. In terms of ritual, it is a very unimpressive ceremony. It seems to be more of a traditional social get-together than any kind of invocation service.

The main activity is beer drinking. Although it never happens, the possibility was suggested that everyone would gather and find there was no beer! "Then the biki would be cancelled and everyone would go home!"

As insignificant as it seems, the Dukkawa are strictly faithful in attending the *Mai-giro biki.*

# EDITORIAL POSTSCRIPT

If Heisenberg's "Uncertainty Principle"[1] has any application to the Social Sciences, and many of us indeed believe that it has, then it is manifest that the best position from which to observe and evaluate the complexities and contradictions of a society such as the Dukkawa represent is that of complete acceptance, and not that of a mere transient outsider. Such a position could quite easily be achieved by a thoughtful and sympathetic Administrative Officer (most especially the more junior ones) in the days of the Colonial Service's apogee of unquestioned authority. Very often it was! Similarly, the missionaries *ought* to have been able to assume an equal point of vantage, though very often they could not bring themselves to do so.

Formal scholarship, as represented by the field researcher, complete with his recorders, index cards, quantitive evaluations etc., etc. has rather more difficulty, and is much more certain to be effected by Heisenberg's principle. The caricature of the Ph. D. candidate in *Little Big Man* was not altogether a caricature, any more than are the only all too familiar airs and affectations immediately adopted by otherwise good and simple people when under the glare of a television camera in a "snap" interview, or as eye witnesses to some catastrophe, less than factual either.

It is therefore Father Prazan's ability to step outside the purely priestly standpoint — unless, indeed the appearance of so doing is not, in itself, the ultimate development of the vocation — which makes his observation of Dukku life so valuable. There *is*

---

[1] That the very act of measuring (or observing) a phenomenon in itself alters the behaviour which is being studied. Werner Karl Heisenberg (1901–1976), advanced this theory initially in regard to pure mathematics and physics, but its application to other disciplines has since become more widely accepted.

200

a place in scholarship for a dedicated amateur, and especially for one to whom the time factor, the need to "beat a deadline" has little or no importance.

There is one area, however, in which throughout this study the Uncertainty Principle may have been at work all the time, and this is in the medium of communication between the author and his informants.

Attention to this problem was drawn in the opening pages, and the question which it poses is still unresolved. But it may be that it is not the serious issue that was first envisaged.

Some cultures resist any encroachment on their language with vigorous reaction against the encroachers, either social or political.[2] The Dukkawa, it seems, may be somewhat less concerned about the enrichment of their language by lexical borrowing than are others, the Editor included! A sample word-list of *Dukkanci* into Hausa has come into my hands and would seem to show that in many respects, the Hausa-ization of the Dukku language has been longstanding, though not pervasive.

The word-list is not extensive, being only 46 in all, but the words themselves are all important ones in that each one pertains to matters which have been identified in the text as having relevance to Dukku mores. With the aid of a colleague who is a distinguished philologist[3] this list has been reduced to the most commonly used symbols of the I. P. A., and analysed in regard first to those words which clearly have their origin in the dominant Hausa culture, and secondly in regard to the societal and cultural norms upon which such words may be expected to have their impact. The list in its entirety is reproduced as pages 204 - 207.

It is entirely to be expected (much as the French purists resent the fact) that "product words" — in this case words like *d'akuwa, fatari, k'osai* and *k'ulik'uli* — should transfer into another language along with the acceptance by the new culture of the

---

[2] Witness the recent outpourings against "Franglais", which have resulted in "le hotdog", "le drugstore" and "les bluejeans" being virtually outlawed. English has not reacted similarly to "détente", "rendezvous", or "fiancé (ée)", though there is a certain *native* resistance to "real" and "good" as adverbs and to "went" instead of "gone"!

[3] I am much indebted to Dr. H.H. Petit, Professor of English at Duquesne University for his assistance in arriving at this analysis.

product they describe. What is remarkable about the words in Group A of the sample now under consideration, therefore, is the inclusion in such a list of "concept words" (really "culture words") such as *bazara, gayya* and, above all in view of the weight that the Dukku culture clearly assigns to their function, *biki*.

Allied to this peculiar circumstance, moreover, is the second group of "product words" such as *kalangu, kalme, kimba* and *turu*. As regards to the words in Group B, the sample is clearly inadequate as a basis from which to offer any opinion.

The first thing to be observed about the last four words quoted, is that they must surely represent a technological improvement which the Dukkawa recognised and accepted, with, as a result, the acceptance also of the nomenclature along with the new technology, in the same way that the products described above were also accepted. In the case of the drums, the improvement discerned would be the difference in performance between the *Ukalangu, Ukimba* and *Uturu* on the one hand, and the *Ilkwia* or *Udum* (possibly) on the other.

Similarly a differentiation of function (or perhaps merely a ready availability at a lesser cost) would apply to the acceptance of the *Ukuhlmi* hoe on the one hand as against the *Ilkundt, Ukete* (possibly) and *Worl* hoes on the other.

The same observations, indeed, might even apply to *bazara*, as a concept, though usually seasons etc., especially in a community so agriculturally oriented as that of the Dukkawa, tend to be recognised *ab initio*, and to be given their own proper names.

But what of *gayya* and *biki*, two words which describe concepts which are fundamental to Dukku sociology?[4]

Can it be that the now central aspects of Dukku social intercourse (for both *gayya* and *biki* describe highly social activities) are relatively recent imports from the Hausa culture?[5]

If so, then how recent has its incorporation been? Twice in the text, Father Prazan identifies shifts in Dukku customs, once in the case of nose tacks *vs* lip-rings, and once in the case of leaves *vs*

---

[4] A third essential concept, *kunya*, though identified with the Hausa word has its own particular description in Dukkanci, *Okiæl*.

[5] Of course, the converse could also be true, though the evidence would have to be persuasive!

cloths for the women. I, for my part, identified one certain "incubation" (the guinea-worm egg filter) and possibly a second (building in sun dried bricks). This last, in particular, would appear to be given weight by the appearance in the sample of a word in Dukkanci for *jan gini* (madamnanæk). Whether any word exists to describe construction with brick remains to be seen, though it would be interesting to suggest that if it does, it could (if the theory set out here does, in fact, operate) well be that it sounds something like *Utuhbuli!*

These, and a host of similar questions arise from Father Prazan's text. Like all good scholarship it inevitably raises more questions than it answers. It is greatly to be hoped, therefore, that he will be given a chance in the not too distant future to apply himself to the solution of some of them.

Whilst what he has done must be applauded, the amount of work that still remains to be done in order to permit us to achieve even a reasonably objective view — let alone an intimate and understanding one — of societies like that of the Dukkawa, is enormous and pressing. Time is fast running out on us!

GROUP A                          *In alphabetical order of Hausa*

*Words in sample clearly associated with*
*"standard" Hausa original. (24%).*

|          |                      | Dukkanci |          |
|----------|----------------------|----------|----------|
| Hausa    | English              | Phonetic | Roman    |
| BAZARA   | HOT SEASON           | ụuazɔ́ra  | UWAZORA  |
| BIKI     | FEAST, PARTY         | ụbɨkʰi    | UBIKI    |
| DAK'UWA  | PEANUT CANDY         | im:dɛkua | IMDEKWA  |
| FATARI   | WOMAN'S LOWER BODYCLOTH | ɨlfatari | ILFATARI |
| GAYYA    | COMMUNAL WORK        | ụ:gæiyã  | UGAENIYAEN |
| KALANGU  | HOUR-GLASS DRUM      | ụkalangụ | UKALANGU |
| KALME    | TILLING HOE          | ụkʌl:mi  | UKUHLMI  |
| KIMBA    | W. AFRICAN PEPPER & A TYPE OF DRUM | ukim:ba | UKIMBA |
| K'OSAI   | BEAN FLOUR CAKE      | il:kuesɛ | ILKWESE  |
| K'ULIK'ULI | PEANUT CRISPS & A CICATRICE PATTERN | kulikuli | KŪLIKŪLI |
| TURU     | KETTLEDRUM           | utʰu:ru   | UTŪRŪ    |

## GROUP B

*Words in sample which may or may not be associated with standard Hausa or a form of it, either wholly or in part. (4%).*

| Hausa | English | Dukkanci Phonetic | Roman |
|-------|---------|-------------------|-------|
| MAFARIN TABA | THE FIRST TOBACCO | tåk$^h$an dụta:ba | *TAKAN DUTĀBA |
| NAMIJIN GIYA | BEER "STARTER" | nʌme:zimimk$^h$ɛ | NUHMEJIM IMK |

---

*Note: — In view of the ubiquity of "taba" in its many and varied forms, no attempt should be made to draw any firm conclusions as to a Hausa origin in this case.

## GROUP C  *In alphabetical order of Dukkanci*

*Words in sample having no connection with a Hausa original. (72%)*

| Hausa | English | Dukkanci Phonetic | Roman |
|-------|---------|-------------------|-------|
| RUMBUN MATA | WOMAN'S STORE | biụdụ mǽeinụ | BIUDU MÁEINU |
| DAWA | SORGHUM | çṹ | CHU |
| MIYA | SAUCE | ɛts̃ɔ́ | ETCHO |
| KWARURU | BAMBARRA PEANUT | guene / mæigirgir | GWENE / MAEGIRGIR |
| FARIN JINI | POPULARITY, ACCEPTANCE | hiụmpụsmɔ | HIUPŪSMO |

| Hausa | English | Phonetic | Roman |
|---|---|---|---|
| RUMBU | CORNBIN, GRANARY | ɨlbiụ | ILBIU |
| TUWO | PORRIDGE | ɨlgʌ́ | ILGUH |
| WASA | PLAY, GAME | ɨlhụjt$^h$e | ILHUYTE |
| MADAFI | KITCHEN AREA | ɨl:k$^h$at$^h$a | ILKATA |
| DUNGA | TILLING HOE | ɨlku:ndt$^h$ | ILKUNDT |
| KURKUTU | DRUM | ɨlkuia | ILKWIA |
| GORMO* | DOWRY SERVICE | ɨlmɔn | ILMON |
| YAKUWA | RED SORRELL | ɨl:piæs | ILPIAES |
| GAUDE | GARDENIA ERUBESCENS | imh$^h$i | IMHI |
| RUWAN TOKA | "ASH WATER" | imkik$^h$ | IMKIK |
| KUNU | GRUEL | imzug: | IMZŪG |
| YAUD'O | CERATO- THECA SESAMOIDES | in:del: | INDEL |
| SARKIN NOMA | HEAD FARMER | k$^h$ojʌmmukʌt$^h$ | KOYUHMMŪKUHT |
| ALLAH | GOD | k$^h$ojʌmmusɨl | KOYUHMMŪSIL |
| SARKIN DAJI | HEAD OF THE HUNTERS | k$^h$ojʌmmut$^h$ʌm | KOYUHMMŪTUHM |
| JAN GINI | "CONSOLI- DATED" METHOD OF BUILDING | madamnanæk | MADAMNANAEK |
| KUNYA | MODESTY | ok$^h$iæl: | OKIAEL |
| WAK'AR GORMO | DOWRY SER- VICE SONG | sept$^h$ilmɔn | SEPTILMON |
| RAMA | HIBISCUS CANNABINUS | ụ:buru | UBŪRŪ |
| GANGA | BIG DRUM | ụ:dum | UDŪM |

Dukkanci

| Hausa | English | Phonetic | Roman |
|---|---|---|---|
| ZANA | LARGE MAT | u̧guʔ | UGWE |
| ZAURE | ENTRANCE HUT | u̧he:j | UHEY |
| TABARMA | SLEEPING MAT | u̧h$^h$uet$^h$ | UHŪET |
| GARMA | PLOUGHING HOE | u̧:k$^h$et$^h$ɛ | UKETE |
| D'AKI | ROUND HUT | u̧k$^h$uru | UKŪRŪ |
| ABOKIN WASA | JOKING FRIEND | u̧æl:gam | WAELGAM |
| IGIYA | STRING, ROPE | u̧he:j: | WHEY |
| FARTANYA | RIDGING HOE | u̧:ɔr:l | WORL |

Note: — The Roman rendition is, of course, only an approximation. The digraph AE is used for the sound of *a* as in *bad*.

ɨ is utilised in the phonetic rendition as the crossed vowel *i*.

Note: This list, obviously, constitutes a very limited sample. Moreover, its inclusion in the text is purely "experimental", in that it is utilised only to illustrate a point. Until a great deal more research is done on this and related questions, therefore, any conclusions should be regarded as being purely tentative. (Ed.)

\* As has been noted in the text, this does not appear to be "standard" Hausa.

# INDEX

Abortion, 135-36
Activities
    men's, 51-63
    women's, 63-65
Animals, domestic, 60-62
Architecture, 29-45
Arm bands, 19-23

Beer, guinea-corn, 64-65
*Biki. See also* Festivals
    *Bikin Shanu,* 173-74
    *Bikin Maharba,* 174-76
    head-farmer's, 164-66
    kinds of, 163-76
    *Mai-Giro,* 172-73
    marriage, 166-72
    minor, 172-76
Birth, 111-117
Blacksmiths, 62
Bodily functions, 104
Bows and arrows, 73-77
Burial Service, 138-45

Calabashes, 46-47
Calf bands, 23
Charms, 188-96
Circumcision, 116-117
Clothing, 14-17, 105
Community living, 26-50
Compound, typical, 28-29
Contraception, 134
Cookery, 63-65
Cooking, 98-101
Cowry beads, 23-25
Crafts, 62-63

Daily routine, 94-110
    afternoon, 96
    late evening, 97
    morning, 94-96
Death, 137-154
Diseases, 81-82. *See also* Medicine
    infectious, 82
    parasitic, 81-82
Domestic life, 86-93
Dowry, 125-27
Drums, 157-63

Earrings, 18
Eating, 101-02
Engagement, 119-21
    greeting, 122

Ethics, sexual and marital, 130-33
Eyes, 19

Facial markings, 17
Family circle, 86-93
    hierarchy of authority, 87-91
Farming, 51-60
    tools, 55-58
Festivals, 155-76. *See also* Biki
Fornication and adultery, 134
Funeral *Biki,* 146-54, 163-64

Granary, construction of, 31-36, 41
Greetings, 105-07
Guest hut, 38-42
Guns, 70-73

Headbands, 17
*Henna,* 23
Hospitality, 107-110
Hunting, 66-80
    trips, 77-80
Huts,
    construction of, 30-31
    personal, 36-41
Hygiene, 102-104

Inheritance, 92-93
Intercourse, 133-34

Kitchen, 38-42

Labor, division of, 51-65
Leather-workers, 62
Lip-rings, 18-19
Location and environment, 3-8

*Mai-Giro* (Lord), 197-99
Marriage, 118-36
    *Biki,* 128-30, 166-72
Mats, 45-46
Medicine(s), 81-85. *See also* Diseases
Mortar and pestle, 46
Mourning, 145-46
    end of, 152-54

Neck wear, 19
Nose tacks, 18

Ornamentation, 17-25

Physical appearance, 9-25

209

# INDEX